"A must read! This book calls me to question my doubts and my fears, to silence the negative thoughts that would make me less."

—Josiah Hawley (Top 10 Finalist on NBC's The Voice)

"This is a great book for singers or anyone wanting to pursue a dream!"

—James David (Featured vocalist on Fox's Glee series)

"I LOVE *The Voice of Your Dreams*! It is both practical, yet Bold, easy to follow, and hard to put down. Relatable and honest, it inspires ACTIONS that you can take *today*.

—James Kyson (Actor: NBC's Heroes, FX's Justified, CBS' Hawaii Five-0, Despicable Me)

"Trade-in 'Someday' for now. *The Voice of Your Dreams* will show you the path!"

—Dane Sanders (Author of Fast Track Photography)

"This book left a deep and lasting impression on me. While the concepts were profound, the delivery was relatable and easy to understand. I will definitely be referencing this book over and over."

—Kelly Johnson (Celebrity Wardrobe Stylist: Jennifer Lopez, Nazanin Boniadi)

"*The Voice of Your Dreams* is a comprehensive look at the voices we choose to follow/listen to as humans. This book offers practical and inspiring life applications on how to

become who we need to be in order to get the results we want in life. It introduces the concept of 'New Dreamers' and gave me real world examples on how to live a fuller, freer life as a New Dreamer."
—Greg Ullery (Style Director at Lucky Brand)

"In *The Voice of Your Dreams*, Aaron demystifies what it means to turn your dreams into reality. He helps us to see that what we believe about ourselves is the key to unlocking the mystery of 'making it'."
—Wayne Miller (Music Director: Christina Perri, Olivia Somerlyn)

"*The Voice of Your Dreams* provides a useful and thought-provoking guide empowering you to reflect on your best and purpose-filled life. Each chapter will challenge you to find meaning in your daily choices while coaching you to discover and strive for your aspirations without limitations. You will be inspired to give yourself permission to become a New Dreamer and to live out your unique dreams today.
—Dr. Shannon M. Taylor (Administrator and Professor, Loyola Marymount University)

"Getting this book is an important first step towards crafting a better inner voice and boldly stepping into your future with confidence. Aaron truly cares about your narrative and helps you change a seemingly overwhelming life to obtainable moments that lead to health and success."
—Joby Harris (Designer and Visual strategist, JPL /NASA)

THE VOICE OF YOUR DREAMS

THE VOICE OF YOUR DREAMS

Turn Down the Voices of Limitation
and Turn Up the Volume of Success

AARON ANASTASI

NEW DREAMERS

For more information contact:
New Dreamers Publishing
www.thevoiceofyourdreams.com

ISBN 978-0-9970351-3-1 (paperback)

Editing by Chelsea Richardson
Cover designed by John Carr & Estée Ochoa
Text design by Dotti Albertine

Printed in the United States of America

for Adrian
who helped me amplify
the voice of my dreams

CONTENTS

CONTENTS

INTRODUCTION

My Story and Why You May Need This Book

Sometimes I have entire conversations with people and don't hear a word they say. At times there's so much chaos in my head that I simply cannot focus on their words. It's not that I don't want to hear them—well, sometimes I probably don't, if I'm honest—but I just can't seem to hone in on what they're saying.

I'm guessing the same might be true for you.

In fact, you can barely even hear me right now.

There's another voice (a conversation, really) in your head that is in competition with these printed words. This voice is incessantly chattering, commentating. If you're thinking to yourself, "Wait a minute, I don't have a voice in my head"—that's the voice I'm talking about.

While we can—and will occasionally—guide the voice, it constantly runs on its own in the background. We've become so used to it, that we usually don't even realize it's there.

This voice may be saying things like, "Is reading this book worth my time?" or, "What am I getting out of this?" or, "Do I need to be a singer to understand and/or get value from this book?" (No, you don't, by the way) or, "Can I actually apply the things this guy is about to say?" or, "I really need to run a load of laundry today if I want clean socks and underwear tomorrow."

While these particular voices are relatively harmless, and could just be considered "thinking," they are evidence of the existence of others—buried beneath the surface—that are far more destructive. These other voices are the ones that don't ever have anything new or novel to say but incessantly repeat the same types of phrases and conversations that limit our possibilities, our creativity, and our successes (relationally, physically, vocationally, financially, and otherwise).

For example, they say things like, "It's never going to work, so why even try?" or, "You're too old to pursue that now. Just give up."

We become so accustomed to these voices that they begin to occur to us as reality, and this so-called "reality" radically affects our day-to-day performance.

And our performance affects the *results* we get in our lives.

These limiting voices have the ability to keep us stuck—estranged from our deepest desires for months, or years even. Worst of all, if we don't interrupt these voices, we could spend the rest of our lives living an uninspiring and unfulfilling existence...a comfortable but zombie-like reality.

But this doesn't have to be the case; there is another option.

The question, "What do you do?" has become more and more difficult for me to answer. What I do with my time and what I do for money are often very different.

Now, some of the things I do simply because I love them become sources of income, but I do them *first* because I love them and *second* as a potential income source.

I went from barely getting by financially, doing work I mostly hated, to making six figures, spending most of my time doing things that I love. I went from a stagnant dating relationship to a fun marriage. I went from completely stuck in my life when it came to pursuing my dreams to beginning to walk them out.

I know this sounds like a fantasy (and maybe even an over-promising, hyped infomercial). You may even be thinking, "Hey, good for you, man. But most of us live in the real world." This transition is not easy, per se, but my guess is that it's much more attainable than you think—and not just for some people, but for *you*.

There is a blueprint; and the practical—and sometimes odd—principles and ways of being in this blueprint are what I will share with you in this book.

Most people, and I include my past self in this generalization, are resigned to a certain way of thinking, believing that life is hard and dreams are fine for kids and teenagers but grinding out a living is just a necessary evil. But the real truth, the truth that I've experienced, is that it is possible to do what makes you feel excited to be alive and also make a good living on it.

In fact, I would argue that it's possible to do exclusively the things that bring you life and make far more money doing so. It has certainly been true for me. While money doesn't necessarily make you happy, happy people tend to make more money and have a far better chance of witnessing the unfolding of their dreams.

I'll show you how to reinvent yourself in such a way that you will wake up in the morning with a sense of anticipation and excitement about what you're up to in the world and how today is an opportunity to build toward something that you really, really, *really* want—a legacy worth living into.

If you've picked up this book, chances are that you feel like you were meant for more, that there is a certain greatness of which you are capable that hasn't quite yet come to fruition. Maybe you've felt a longing or tension that you were created to do something in the world that matters— that you were created to do far more than simply exist and survive. If that's the case for you, then this book is the roadmap that will help you get there.

How? It begins with a simple distinction that most people fail to see, something that I failed to see for the better part of my life. I had times of accidentally, sporadically stumbling onto it, but it wasn't until I fully discovered it, fleshed it out, and learned to intentionally apply it to my life that I experienced a quantum change. This sudden, dramatic, and enduring transformation permeated through and improved *every* area of my life.

Our way of *being* is the primary factor that determines the results we get in life, *not* our actions. Most people think they need to shift what they're doing or the amount of self-discipline they have in order to be more successful and/or reach their dreams. This is only one small part of it; until we win the battle in the mind (our limiting voices) and take control of our ways of being, our actions will be rendered virtually powerless. Until we shift our ways of *being*, no amount of *doing* will produce different results, since those actions are still coming out of the same framework that keeps us stuck in the first place.

In order to infuse our actions with power, we must discover and redesign the hidden thoughts and beliefs that are automatically driving our behavior. Once we do this the quality of our actions changes, the place we're coming from changes, and these shifts create radical, lasting transformations in every area of our lives.

We are aware of some of our thoughts and beliefs that keep us stuck—our limiting voices—while others hold us back without us even realizing they're there. These voices are so much a part of our daily lives that we tend to relate to the hidden ones as if they're undeniably true. We say things like, "That's just the way things are," or, "It is what it is," or, "That's just who I am."

One line of thinking I discovered, which is particularly insidious for me is, "I don't have what it takes," or in other words, "I'm not enough; there's something inherently wrong with me." These are some (but definitely not all) of the primary limiting voices that kept me from moving toward my dreams for years.

It may help to know where this all started for me.

The Catalyst for Writing This Book

I remember several years ago sitting with my life coach, and I was complaining about how difficult it was to break into the music and film industry. I was completely stuck and depressed, frustrated and angry that life didn't seem to be working for me no matter how hard I tried. I seemed to be getting the same results over and over again; every time I was on the cusp of a great opportunity coming to fruition, it was like the rug was pulled out from under me. I lived with the dull, soggy feelings of self-doubt, hurt, shame, and regret. I was stuck and had been for years.

After I was done complaining to my coach he asked me who I would have to *be* (not what I'd have to do) to get the results I wanted. This question detonated inside of me with a powerful force.

You see, I had thought I simply needed to work harder in order to get unstuck. But that strategy was simply increasing my level of despair. What I really needed was a new way of being; I needed to redesign my thoughts and beliefs—I needed to reframe of the context in which I was approaching my actions.

So this contrast between *being* and *doing* began a journey for me, a search that helped me answer the question that was plaguing me:

"How do I get the results I want in life?"

I answered that question for myself, and this book will answer it for you. I will show you exactly how to move toward the greatest version of *you*, away from comfort and safety and toward a life of adventure, excitement, peace, and fulfillment.

How on earth did I go from living fearfully and being stuck relationally, financially, and vocationally to being in a great marriage, quadrupling my income, and working only a few hours a week on income-producing endeavors while spending the rest of my time doing only the things that are exciting to me? Again, it's simpler than you think, and this book will show you how (suspend disbelief for at least a few chapters).

Confessions

I'm not special. I don't come from money or prestige—far from it. I grew up on the wrong side of the tracks with a father who worked long hours to bring home near-poverty wages—and those were the "prosperous" years before the divorce. Neither of my parents went to college, and only one graduated from high school. I personally have failed at so many endeavors in my life that still today I continue to battle the limiting voices in my head that repeat things like, "You *are* a failure, and therefore you'll never have sustained success," and, "There is something inherently wrong with you. Pursing your dream? What a joke. Who are you trying to kid? Just stop. You're embarrassing yourself."

My Promise

Look, I just stumbled on some principles that altered the course of my life. And the truth is that I don't always apply them, but to the degree that I do, I see radical results over time—and I mean *radical*.

The steps and strategies in this book can be used to attain incredible results; whether you're stuck in your life or you're already crushing it and are ready for the next big challenge—the next step toward your dreams. This book will show you how to see and take hold of options and opportunities that most people won't.

New Dreamers

There is an emerging underground culture that is taking hold of a life they previously considered impossible. They are called "New Dreamers." These New Dreamers are replacing their previous assumptions, implementing these principles, and turning their dreams into concrete realities.

New Dreamers (**ND**) are not like the traditional dreamers, "Old Dreamers" (**OD**), whose dreams are still in the realm of fantasy, while they soothe themselves with the "someday" lie. New Dreamers are tired of that lie and are committed to the realization of their deepest desires and their highest selves.

Here are a few of the differences between New Dreamers and Old Dreamers:

OD: Live reactively, out of their automatic responses, which continually produce the same unwanted results. Circumstances dictate their destiny.

ND: Identify their limiting voices and live out their commitments instead. They are the authors of their own futures.

OD: Wish, hope, and long for things to happen, without the type of passion—the willingness to suffer for a dream—that turns those things into reality. They choose certain actions, seeking to become what they hope to be, but often find themselves discouraged in the face of perceived roadblocks…and quit, or stay stuck.

ND: Choose to *be* what they most desire to be and let their actions be a natural outworking of who they declare they are. They don't give up, because they can't cease to be who they are.

OD: Fear of looking like a failure, which often keeps them stuck and out of action.

ND: Understand that failure is not a *problem* they will ever face but that it is the actual *pathway* to greatness.

OD: Get overwhelmed by how much work it's going to take to turn this dream into a reality.

ND: Take the tiniest steps each day, knowing that success is a natural byproduct of staying on the path and staying in action toward accomplishing the next small project that is leading toward this huge dream.

What Makes this Book Different?

This is a different kind of how-to or self-help book. It doesn't lay out the nuts and bolts of how to build a successful business or how to have better relationships (although that is most often a natural result of applying these principles) or how to make it as a singer (or actor or entrepreneur or coach or dentist or whatever you want to be).

No, it's much more than that.

Using New Dreamer techniques, this book explains how to *be* the kind of person that is successful in whatever you do. You'll learn about how to change your ways of *being* that turn up the volume of success in *every* area of your life.

The voice of your dreams is calling to you, but it can be difficult to hear when the voices of limitation are shouting so much louder—especially as you embark on new challenges and new relationships. But there is a way to quiet them, to silence them, and to allow your deeper purpose to emerge. And this book will show you exactly how to do that.

A Short Case Study of One New Dreamer

John is a writer/director who was stuck in his latest attempt of raising money, sitting in the shame of his failed crowd-funding campaign. He had raised only $14,000 of his $60,000 goal for his short film—a film he was passionate about because its purpose was to raise funds and awareness to help stop sex trafficking. A short time after he hired me as a coach and began applying these New Dreamer principles he not only reached his original goal but also raised a total of $80,000 for the project. He made the film and—much more than that—reinvigorated his sense of possibility. A few months later he also won a CMA (Country Music Association) Award for directing the music video of the year.

Join the Movement

Every person alive has a voice of their dreams that calls to them. Some will identify with this statement right away. But others are not able to hear this voice anymore after years and years of discarding it as "unrealistic" or "impractical."

The good news is that that voice hasn't stopped speaking, and we can tap back into it anytime we choose. And when we do, we take the first step toward joining the community of New Dreamers.

Join the New Dreamer movement and take your dreams out of the "someday" category and turn them into a project that you can begin working toward *today*.

PART 1

GETTING STARTED

1
Where to Start

"Well begun is half done."
~ARISTOTLE

The most common place where singers, actors, writers, entrepreneurs, and other creatives get stuck is "where to start." This isn't just a roadblock for the beginner pursuing an endeavor for the first time; the "where to start" question can strike at any step in the process and on any—or potentially every—given day.

This is one of the reasons Ernest Hemingway always stopped his writing session for the day with one idea left to write about—so that he would have a place to start writing again the following day. Hemingway knew that more ideas would emerge as he sat down to do the work. *Starting* was the primary "stuck" place that he was determined to work through. Hemingway was a New Dreamer; he understood this principle of action that often escapes us. Inspiration and passion most often arise while we're in action, getting busy doing whatever it is that we insist we want to do so badly. Sitting and waiting for inspiration to strike reveals a misunderstanding of this truth. The inspiration we're waiting for before we start is on the other side of starting.

While inspiration can sometimes strike when you're not in action, it's generally a sporadic and unreliable system to count on if you want to accomplish your goals. Usually the best place to begin is...well, anywhere. I know that sounds silly, but it's the truth. Once we're in action the path toward our goals opens and inspiration begins to bubble up inside of us.

New Dreamers commit to a few minutes at a time, or less, even. This small commitment gets us into action. It could be five vocal exercises or three minutes trying to figure out a song on guitar or writing two hundred words on a new book.

Let success be defined as completion of a small goal you set for yourself each day. These goals add up, eventually putting you on the path toward the future that you're creating, which will become a future worth having and living into.

John Wooden, as the head coach of UCLA's basketball team in the 1960s and 1970s, won more national championships than anyone else in history. In his words, "When you improve a little each day, eventually big things occur."

So many of us get stuck thinking we need to make a running leap into our future. In reality, great futures are formed little by little in the present moment. Focusing too much on the future while in the present moment leads to anxiety—another way to get stuck. Setting up short-term goals that allow you to feel accomplished each day leads to the motivation to continue on with your long-term goals. There's no need to hold your happiness hostage to the accomplishment of the big, far-off goal. You can allow yourself to feel great about accomplishing something today that will eventually lead to the end result you desire. This is how success comes—for everyone.

Part of the trick is to redefine what success means to you. Yes, accomplishing the end goal is one way to define success, but that thinking doesn't always serve you while you're in the process of working towards it. Earl Nightingale, a famous speaker and author in the 1950s, said it like this: "Success is the progressive realization of a worthy goal or ideal." The primary operative term for me here is *progressive*. Success is staying on the path toward your goal, little by little. So if you're on the path, you're already achieving success, whereas getting out of action temporarily puts the brakes on success.

When I say "success" I don't just mean financial or career success but any goal you have in any area, whether relational, physical, vocational, financial, or in terms of attaining your dreams. Small, consistent action is always how we get there.

Another reason New Dreamers implement small actions while working toward a larger end goal is because the mind makes all future tasks seem bigger and scarier than they really are. This is the reptilian part of the brain thinking it's helping you survive by being prepared for the worst-case scenario. This evolutionary defense mechanism doesn't serve you when you're seeking to accomplish your goals in the modern day. And because these future tasks seem scary, we tend to procrastinate. This makes getting into action even scarier, while adding in shame—some "I should have" and "I've really got to" and maybe even a dose of, "What's the use? I'm never going to see this through; who am I trying to kid?"

When we get into action, even three or five minutes at a time, we begin seeing the task differently. It's not as "impossible" as it previously appeared. The whole endeavor presents itself to us differently.

Take, for example, the writing of this book. As I begin, many of these limiting voices attempt to take center stage in my mind: "Nobody cares what you have to say," and, "Who do you think you are to write a book?" and, "You'll never finish, and even if you do nobody will ever read it."

Believing these and other similar voices kept me from writing this book for years. Even once I finally decided to do so and put it in my schedule, I thought, "Well, my desk needs to be clean first." By the time I finished straightening up and cleaning the living room, kitchen, and closet, it was time for lunch. After lunch I finally sat down with half the day gone. After sitting down I thought, "I'll just check and see if anyone 'liked' my Facebook post from earlier."

I didn't write a single word that day, but I did eat an entire quart of ice cream that night.

I discovered that I can't actually eat my fears, but I was willing to give it a valiant effort.

The next day went similarly.

So today I decided that ten minutes of writing would *be* success—as I define it. I gave myself a pep talk and drummed up the courage to sit down and write a couple of words. And you know the crazy thing? I've been writing today for more than two hours, and I feel invigorated. Once I got into it, I remembered how much I really do love to write.

Stephen King's words ring true for me when he says, "The scariest moment is always just before you start." So, what can you start right now? Just for a few minutes. Allow yourself to get past that scariest moment and into the rewarding joy of action.

Because well begun is half done.

For my students and clients there is usually one main thing that they know would have a radical impact toward accomplishing their goals, if they put some time into it. What might that thing be for you right now? Take a moment to think about it. That thing that is coming to mind right now—that you may be avoiding—are you willing to put down this book and spend three minutes working on it? After three minutes you could stop—if you can stop, that is. Once you get going and realize it's maybe not as hard as you had imagined, you're less inclined to stop.

It might be your daily vocal exercises or learning a new chord on guitar. It could be reaching out to the person who you know could help you take the next step toward getting back on the path of success as it relates to your dreams.

Join the New Dreamer movement, beginning with one small action today.

2

But... What If I Fail?

"Success is stumbling from failure to failure
with no loss of enthusiasm."
~WINSTON CHURCHILL

When I first created my singing program, Superior Singing
Method, it was a massive failure, by anybody's estimation.
It was actually called "The Singing Guide" back then. My
business partners and I had spent nearly two years building
the company, but when we finally launched the program, it
didn't hit. In fact, it completely flopped.

So this was a major setback at the time, and I had a
choice to make. Was this what I really wanted, or is this
failure enough to pack it up, tell myself I gave it my best
shot, and move on?

Now, I don't want to move past this part too quickly
and give some swift solution of how I may have overcome
this challenge. This place of sitting in the wake of failure
is painful, right? This is the place where many people find

themselves all the time—that is, if they haven't yet made it their life goal to play small and be sure to avoid any more big risks and failures in life, like I did for so long. There's a lot to contend with in our minds when we find ourselves here.

In fact, if you're anything like me, some of the limiting voices of long-past failures still scream out years and years later. Maybe they say something like, "I told you this wasn't going to work out," or, "You're so stupid; you should have known better," or, "You got too big for your britches, didn't you?" (If you've never been to the South, then the word "britches" may not yet be in your vocabulary, but you get the idea).

I was devastated. I had had high hopes for what the project could possibly be, but instead it seemed that it was just a colossal waste of time—two years down the drain. I was really embarrassed to tell anyone about it, so I didn't. I felt ashamed.

After moping around for a few days (alright, fine...a few weeks) I spent some time thinking through what my vision was for this business and why I wanted to create it in the first place. What had compelled me to spend all that time working on it while working other part time jobs just to pay my bills?

After some soul-searching I realized that I am passionate about helping others live fuller, freer lives, and that everything I do is filtered through that strong desire. One major part of what invigorates me about that is helping people work toward attaining their dreams.

New Dreamers understand that they are always in a better position to make a contribution when aligning work with their values, so for me it became more about that core value to serve than any other benefits—like passive income and having a great job and so on. Those things are great (really great!), but understanding what drives me at the core helped me to see this not as a failure but simply a set-back, a learning experience, and one more step along the way toward an endeavor in which I'm determined to succeed because so much more is now at stake.

This experience helped me realize that this is who I am at a core level; thus, I couldn't fail at being who I am or who I choose to be. That was impossible. New Dreamers define who they are and what they're up to on the outset, so whatever they do is an outworking of who they are—not an attempt to define their identity.

I took this "failure" as information to help me formulate a new plan that would bring me closer to my goal and get me back into action. Once we find what it is that we love—singing, acting, writing, creating small businesses, whatever it is—we do it because it gives us life, joy, peace, and passion, and it's in these spaces that we become successful. There is no "failure." What we might see as a "failure" is just the next step in the process of getting further along toward our goals.

Once I got my courage back and made the decision to do whatever it would take to make this business successful, I spent several weeks brainstorming what could be better about the program. I realized that I hadn't yet really created my own method and that the quality and branding left something to be desired. So I spent a year reading more books on singing and really thinking through what genuinely worked for me. I worked steadily for another year before releasing the new and improved Superior Singing Method, with higher quality videos, a method that was all my own, and far better branding. It was a painful (and fun!) journey, and it ended up paying off.

Fast-forward to the present, some years later, and Superior Singing Method (SSM) has become wildly successful—financially, yes; passive income, yes; but more importantly, tens of thousands of people all over the world are closer to reaching their dreams because of it. I've found that this is what feeds my soul, gives me life, and reinvigorates my enthusiasm, in turn generating more fertile ground where opportunity and success can thrive.

You see, when you shift the place that you are coming from—who you're *being*—failure presents itself to you differently. You can now give up all those stories about how you *are* a failure. As author Zig Ziglar says, "Remember, failure is an event, not a person." No person is a failure.

And so, what if I hadn't pushed forward? What if I had let that "failure" stop me in my tracks? What would I have missed out on? What would others have missed out on? What would my family have missed out on?

Is there something you're considering giving up? What is it that you could continue to push through and potentially change your life and others' lives along the way? As a singer, what might the world miss out on if you choose not to practice today and tomorrow and eventually give up, convincing yourself of the falsehood that there is such a thing as natural talent, and that you don't have it?

New Dreamers understand that failure is not a *problem* that we will ever face; it is actually how we achieve our goals. The more we slow down the rate of failure in our lives, the more we slow down the rate of success. The one begets the other. So, fail forward. We're all on the journey of stumbling from failure to failure, and it's those who don't lose enthusiasm or give up who achieve success.

I remember when I had just turned fourteen years old, and I had been playing guitar for about a year or so, but hadn't worked on my singing voice, so I was a little hesitant when the leader of a youth group I was attending asked me if I would be willing to lead the songs at the beginning of all the gatherings. I was, of course, really excited about the opportunity because there was nothing I loved more than playing music, and it was my dream to be a singer-songwriter in a band. So I agreed to lead for an upcoming gathering to see how it went and then go from there. I picked out the songs I would play and practiced and practiced, but I was concerned about how bad my voice sounded—it was horrible. I could play guitar well enough, but my singing, to me, sounded like a dying animal.

The day of the gathering finally came, and I sat down and strummed the chords of the first song and then just went for it and sang out. As I looked around the room (a big mistake), I could see the faces of the other teenagers grimacing, as if to say, "Why the hell is this guy leading the singing?" But I pressed on and got through the rest of that song as well as the others I had prepared.

When I was done playing I remember thinking to myself, "Well, that was a disaster. Not only am I not going to play here next week, I may never be able to show my face around here again." I stuck around for the rest of the gathering, not wanting to be rude. While many avoided eye contact with me, one guy said, "Hey, thanks for playing. It's nice to have music."

They invited me back the following week. I was done licking my wounds and was excited to play again. I was still terrible the following week—more like the following couple of years, but over time I got better.

I continued to play there all through high school and it was actually during that time that I began putting together the pieces of what it took to build my singing voice from terrible to eventually singing professionally, and those principles are what eventually became the foundation for the techniques and exercises of my singing program.

One important New Dreamer principle I learned

during that time was that success comes from a willingness to endure the tension of sucking at something long enough for the breakthroughs to emerge. And trust me, I sucked for a very long time. Most people quit before those breakthroughs have a chance to take place because it's an extremely uncomfortable space to be in. I know all too well; I'm terribly uncomfortable right now as I learn (and suck at) improv—I'm laughably bad, but not the kind of laughter that you're looking for.

The other thing I realized is that I didn't fear failure as much as I feared looking like a failure in front of others. If I try to sing along to a song and squawk out a sour note while I'm at home by myself, I don't mind at all. But if I do the same on stage, now that's a different feeling altogether. Part of the reason I'm taking improv right now is to help curb that part of me that is terrified of looking dumb in front of others. Former professional baseball player Lou Brock says, "Show me a guy who's afraid to look bad, and I'll show you a guy you can beat every time." I don't want to be the guy that gets beaten every time.

As an aside, being a New Dreamer isn't some sort of ascent to an enlightened state where all your actions reflect that of the New Dreamer ideal. We know intuitively that often times our emotions, egos, and fears will stand in the way of reaching the New Dreamer summit on every project and every occasion. Being a New Dreamer is a commitment to live according to a set of principles and ideas that yield the results we want most in life. But there is always room to fail and get back onto the New Dreamer path. In fact, it's expected and is part of being a New Dreamer.

I'm with you. I'm striving daily to continue to become more and more of a New Dreamer. I still fail often, like today when I spent forty five minutes on social media intentionally avoiding working on this chapter because I let discouragement sink in after hearing some feedback I got from a friend on what I had written so far. I'm back on track now—back on the path—but that certainly will not be the last derailment.

And that's okay.

New Dreamers understand that no matter what is going on, there is always room for another chance. Second chances are infinitely available to the New Dreamer. There is always a future hope. Always.

Can you target any area in your life where you're playing safe, not taking a risk for fear of failure? Instead, are you willing to move toward a particular minor goal of yours until you "fail"? Two things are likely to happen. First, you'll be surprised how difficult it is to fail, and second, once you do "fail" you'll discover key pieces of information or inspiration that will clarify what the next, most resourceful step will be. Once a goal comes to mind, would you be willing to write it down and execute it by the end of the day, or better yet, right now?

3

What Do You Want?

"Where there is no vision,
there is no hope."
~George Washington Carver

One of the foundational questions I ask all of my coaching clients is, "What do you want?" I was surprised to find that many people don't know the answer. Some have vague ideas about what they want, but getting clear and specific about what they really, really want is painful for the majority of them.

There can often be a certain fear surrounding the act of admitting to ourselves and others what it is that we really want. That dream in our heart is so dear and precious that it can be difficult to express, for fear that it won't survive the potential ridicule of others.

I know that for me it was easy to vocalize certain dreams of mine, like being a singer, while others—being a life coach (there are many names for what I do, like "success coach" or "executive coach") and an actor and an author— carried a heavier weight of fear. I believed I didn't have what it takes to be those things, so I figured it was obvious to everybody else that I was a fraud with glaring gaps of insufficiency. Therefore, I thought it would be better if I just kept those dreams to myself, which kept me from pursuing them.

For other clients of mine it wasn't so much that they were scared to say what it was that they wanted; instead, they remained vague so that they wouldn't feel as disappointed if their dreams didn't come to pass. They also didn't feel any sense of accountability to accomplish their visions, so they could stay safe when they wanted to avoid moving toward them. I was very familiar with this strategy of avoidance myself, as I used to employ it often.

Yes, I'm very familiar with this unclear path—and it *is* a path. Choosing to remain vague and not clearly articulating our wants and dreams seems like a small, isolated decision, something that we can put off until later, but it's actually a path—one that will not lead to the fulfillment of our dreams and desires. Dreams don't come about on accident; they result from intention.

The truth is, we all already have visions for our lives. It may be to not have a vision at all or to have a vision small enough that we can manage it safely.

One of my clients, whom I'll call Jonathan, had been successful and felt like his life was pretty much set. Jonathan made good money, was married, and had a good community, but something that he couldn't quite put his finger on felt missing to him. With some exploration, we found this hidden dream of becoming a public speaker that he had discounted; it seemed unrealistic. As we continued to look deeper, we found that this exceptionally intelligent man feared that he wouldn't have anything new or valuable to say, that he would be laughed off the stage. So, for years he coasted on his previous success without creating a new, exciting, and a bit scary vision that would wake him back up and make him feel more alive again.

Your vision can be something big, like being a pop star who out sells Taylor Swift, or it can be simple, like being on time to work-related events. One of my simple visions that guides me day-to-day is making my wife laugh three to five times a day. I realize that I have a tendency to be pretty serious and intense, and I know she loves to laugh, so, with this vision of mine, I work to maintain a certain amount of levity and a sense of play in the household and in the relationship.

I also have larger scale visions, which are not necessarily more important. I want to be the number one box office star in Hollywood and be a *New York Times* best-selling author and be the most highly sought after coach in the world. I shudder a little bit after writing these down, because of my own concerns about what my readers will think of me or the possibility of being perceived as a failure if I don't fulfill these dreams—which brings up the next important principle.

Getting clear about what we want and setting a goal to make it happen are not necessarily about accomplishing the exact goal you set as your vision. Now, to be sure, accomplishing the goal is far more likely if you do have a clear vision of what it is, but the more important thing is what that goal does for you—how it focuses the actions you take on a day-to-day basis. There is no shame in not hitting an exact goal. It's really fun when you do, and you often will, but notice how setting the clear goal or vision erupts a new vigor into your life along with a new sense of purpose and challenge.

I remember when my wife and I decided to get out of debt. We were thirty thousand dollars in debt. When I say "we" I really mean that *I* made a series of bad financial decisions when I was younger and brought the debt into the marriage, so it was now *ours*. I had been weighed down by that debt for over a decade, feeling victimized by it, not realizing that I could be done with it if I got a really clear vision and went after it with a different level of intensity.

So, we picked a date that was nine months away and said that we'd be out of debt by that day. We told a handful of people, wrote down the date, and got busy making that vision come to pass.

Now, it wasn't easy. I don't want to blow past the struggle too quickly here. The process felt very confining at times, and we made a lot of sacrifices along the way. While most of our friends were going out and going on trips, we chose to focus on the end goal and how it would feel to be completely debt-free.

We didn't hit our goal of being out of debt by our target date, but we didn't beat ourselves up about it. We simply set a new date and got busy working toward it. Here's the thing—we were ninety five percent out of debt by her birthday and were able to pay the rest off within the following two weeks because of what the goal did for us. It wasn't about meeting the exact date; it was about getting a clear vision of what we wanted and going after it together.

One goal that many of my singing students often express is the desire to sing higher notes or notes in songs that they aren't currently able to sing. This is a great goal. So, now let's make it more precise. How about, "By November 15th, I want to sing half an octave higher than I can sing now." Now, it's a clear, measurable goal—a new vision. New Dreamers understand that the more clear and specific a goal is, the more likely it is to come to pass.

What kind of vision would you like to set for yourself? Would you like to have a band in the next six to eight weeks? Would you like to sing at the House of Blues by the end of the year or sell out the Staples Center in Los Angeles? Would you like to launch a new business before the end of the year? Would you like to have a closer relationship with a family member or friend by intentionally setting a time to call them and go out once a week or maybe once a month?

Hope and purpose become infused into us when we have visions for the different areas of our lives. And I don't mean the kind of hope that is a longing for something that you don't have. That kind of hope can lead us to neglect the beautiful opportunity all around us. This kind of hope is not generally resourceful because it keeps our mindsets in the future and often outside of action.

New Dreamers choose a more resourceful form of hope, one that gives a disposition of possibility and confidence that the small tasks today will lead to a future worth having—a hope that is rife with opportunity in the present. This is the kind of hope that a vision can produce.

I challenge you to take three minutes right now and write down at least one vision to which you would like to commit yourself.

4

I Don't Have What It Takes

"If you hear a voice within you say 'you cannot paint,'
then by all means paint,
and that voice will be silenced."
~Vincent Van Gogh

The common limiting voice, "I don't have what it takes," is a big part of what keeps people stuck and keeps them incessantly seeking permission and approval. We may not use this phrase outright, of course, because it would be tough to think well of ourselves if we did. So, instead it will often appear in the form of a complaint.

For example, when I was avoiding pursuing a career as an actor and filmmaker, this core belief of mine was hidden behind a few basic complaints and a few limiting internal conversations: "It's notoriously hard to break into that industry," or, "It's all about who you know or who you are related to in the industry."

If we zoom out on this idea that we don't have what it takes, we can see that it's most likely the result of an unexamined belief system. We can't know whether we have what it takes unless we spend time and effort pursuing it, and I certainly wasn't—and sometimes still don't, that is, when I revert back to taking these voices at their word. When this is the case I find myself feeling content to have these thoughts stop me in my tracks, giving me an excuse to avoid taking risks. But once I get busy on the road of the daily tasks of being an actor and filmmaker I remember that wondering if I do or don't have what it takes isn't a productive thought that will lead me toward the success that I desire.

There is a possible shift of mind here called *capacity*. New Dreamers ask themselves whether they have the capacity to find the resources they need to be successful. That's a more productive thought—a question that will serve us better when it comes to accomplishing our goals.

So, it's not a question of whether I have what it takes to be successful doing this or that, which usually makes me feel depressed or defeated; it's a question of my resourcefulness and my tenacity. This question takes me out of the victim mindset and puts the ball back into my court. Then I can ask myself a follow up question: "Am I willing to commit to finding the resources I need and doing whatever it takes to be successful at this?"

If the answer is "no," it's not a problem. But at least now I can get out of the shame of saying, "I don't have what it takes," and get back into the position of power, understanding that this is a choice of mine, rather than something that is out of my control. If the answer is "yes," then I ask myself, "What is the smallest possible step that I can take to get myself onto the path of realizing this worthy ideal?" And then I take that step.

If you hear a voice within you say, "I can't sing," or, "I can't act," or, "I can't start a small business," then take action—take the first step—and that voice will be silenced.

What *can* you do? "I can research a new piece of music to learn," or, "I can sign up for a new acting class," or, "I can draft up a business plan." Given your current resources, what can you do now?

Are you willing to write down one action right now that will silence those limiting thoughts? Maybe it's doing your vocal exercises today or choosing to do them daily every morning as part of your morning routine. If you want to act, maybe it's time to begin setting aside money for some headshots. If you want to dance, maybe it's time to look into local dance studios that offer classes. Whatever is coming to mind for you right now—are you willing to do it?

5

What About the Fear Factor?

""Always do what you are afraid to do."
~RALPH WALDO EMERSON

All fear comes from contemplating the future. Unless you're being chased by a bear right in this moment, fear isn't actually a present reality for you, even though it may feel like it.

Most people spend so much time fixating on the future while in the present moment that fear has a way of paralyzing them. We think about how things might go wrong, how people will perceive us, and how others could shame us. We worry that we could be laughed at and ridiculed if we open our mouths to sing or speak.

We can always handle the present moment, but no one can handle something that is merely a projection of the mind; no one can handle the future.

Fear stems from a thought or a belief, even though it *feels* like its source is real and concrete. So, fear becomes a stuck place for us that generally leads to inaction. And we could live our entire lives in this place.

Many do.

The best way to get rid of fear in the moment is to do whatever it is that you're afraid of doing. I know this may sound simplistic and maybe even seem insensitive, but notice what happens when you choose to take action.

First of all, almost immediately, the fear begins to shrink, courage rises, and you get a little bit of an adrenaline jolt. And then as you get into the process of taking action, it not only seems less scary than it previously appeared, but it also feels fun and exciting. All of a sudden you feel alive.

And there is one step beyond this, too. As we continue to do the things we're afraid to do, the fear diminishes more and more over time. While it may not be true for every person and in every endeavor, many times the fear will disappear completely as we continue to engage with it.

I remember when I first began to sing in front of others. I was really nervous—genuinely afraid—as I recounted to you in an earlier chapter. I was afraid of how I would look, if I would stay on key, and how others would perceive me if I sounded terrible. In my mind, I would cease to exist if I messed up; I wouldn't be able to handle it if I blew it.

Fast forward to now, and I can stand up in front of thousands of people and sing with very little fear, mostly just feeling love and play and fun. But this has taken time. I'm older now and have played thousands of gigs with varying crowd sizes all over the country and even the world. Now, there is still a certain amount of nervousness and excitement—and of course some residue of caring what others will think of me if I mess up, but I don't mind too much because it reminds me that singing is still important to me, that it is still an adventure.

There is one other little secret, a shift of mind, used by New Dreamers. When we shift the focus from ourselves and onto the *end user* of what we are creating, it begins to occur to us differently.

If you're a singer, think about what you can potentially provide as a service to the listener. Can you give them a moment of feeling alive and escaping the tyranny of their own thoughts and fears? Would it be possible that you could inspire them to go forward and pursue their dream as a singer? Even if your performance isn't perfect, your very courage to step onto the stage could be enough to inspire someone else to do likewise.

This is especially powerful when part of our fear revolves around feelings of unworthiness, that is, feeling you're not worthy to do whatever it is your dream may be. I know that I came face to face with this feeling when I started coaching. Interestingly enough, it happened both times I chose to be a coach.

About seven years ago is when I decided to be a vocal coach and start my online course and YouTube pages. My feelings of unworthiness were off the charts. I didn't think I was qualified. I thought I would be laughed off the Internet, exposed for the fraud I really felt I was. But once people's lives began to change, and people all over the world began to accomplish their dreams, there was a huge shift of mind for me. It wasn't about me and my little fear of whether others would think I was worthy; it was about the love and service I could provide for people all over the world.

Then, as I mentioned earlier, I decided to be a success coach, working with high-achievers that were already making some type of impact in the world, and here came all those fears of unworthiness, flooding back. Along the way, I noticed that I often felt paralyzed and unequipped, but when I chose to shift the focus away from myself and my own insecurities (sometimes I had to do so daily—or hourly!) onto serving my client, the fear began to take a backseat again. The fear wouldn't go away for good, but would subside enough in the moment for me to show up with a goal to serve as best as I could.

Still today, even though I've seen plenty of objective results in my clients' lives, I often times feel like a fraud. In fact, I was just talking to one of my clients this morning, who I'll call David. He was living in despair when we first started working together. His life was a chaotic mess, in his own words. His career was stalled out and unfulfilling, and he was at the point where he was saying to himself, "What's the point? Why should I go on living in this constant cycle of pain, addiction, and hopelessness?" He was hurt deeply by the recklessness of a few of his past

girlfriends and how they treated his heart, and he was acting out by treating other girls in the same way. We worked
together for months questioning his thoughts and assumptions and applying some of these New Dreamer principles.
It didn't happen overnight, but fast-forward to today, six
months later, and he's a completely new person. He's at
peace with himself and his life, he just negotiated and
closed a multi-million dollar commercial real estate deal,
and has gone from casual serial dating to a committed relationship with a woman he loves and deeply respects.

But, in spite of this and other similar stories, I still
wonder at the outset of a coaching call if I'm going to be
of any help at all to my client. I think about my past and
my own myriad of failures, which can begin to put me in
a low mood of self-doubt and insecurity. But once I shift
my focus off of myself and off of how I might look or how
I might be put to shame, something happens. When I get
out of my own head and get into the world of the end
user (the client, in this case) fear begins to dissipate. As I
focus all of my faculties on how I can serve the person in
front of me, my fear is replaced by love—love for the person and love for the process. And once I'm in action doing
the thing I love, being a contribution to the world, fear
almost ceases to be an issue at all.

Does the fear come back? Unfortunately, it often does.
When I choose to listen to the limiting voices in my head,
the fear returns. But now I—and other New Dreamers like

you—have a secret weapon against fear. Focus on the other, the end user. Get into action by contributing to the person in front of you and to the world.

If we get busy doing what scares us, we move past the scariest part of the entire endeavor. This is because the most potent part of fear is what we *imagine*, not the thing itself. It's never as scary as the mind projects that it will be—never.

Are you willing to start doing whatever it is that you are currently avoiding? What are you afraid of?

I find that the thing I am the most afraid to do is what will lead to the greatest breakthrough for me and for others. And the thing that I'm most afraid to do is the thing that I need to do most. It often leads to some unexpected result that puts me closer to the dream or goal that I desire above all.

Are you afraid you won't be able to sing well? Enroll in a singing course. Are you afraid you won't be a great painter? Buy some paint supplies and find a painting class. Are you afraid you don't have anything valuable to say, so you choose not to write, even though people have told you that you're good with words? Me too. Write, read, or take a creative writing class. Silence the voice of fear by taking action and progressively becoming what you're afraid you cannot become.

PART 2

BEING
vs.
DOING

6

To Be or Not To Be?

"What we can or cannot do,
what we consider possible or impossible,
is rarely a function of our true capability.
It is more likely a function of our beliefs
about who we are."
~Tony Robbins

One major shifting point for me when it comes to being stuck versus having success was a simple question my coach asked: "Who would you have to *be* in order to accomplish your goal of having a career as an actor?" It's a profound question with several layers, so let's spend some time unpacking it.

My first thought was that he misspoke. He must have meant to say, "What would I have to *do*?" right?

Nope, he meant what he said.

What I realized that day, as he began to lay it out for me, was that there was a big misunderstanding in the way I was approaching the pursuit of my dreams. I was so focused on what I needed to *do* to get the things that I wanted, that I was either spinning my wheels and not getting very far or choosing to do nothing at all. I would be feeling discouraged about what the "correct" action might be or by the fact that somehow my life didn't seem to be working, that I wasn't getting the results I really wanted.

This *way of being* idea seemed odd. How can I be anything different from what I already am? I'm being just who I am. I don't have any other choice…right?

Interestingly enough, as an actor—which I've been since I was a kid—the answer was right under my nose. I became characters different from who I am all the time. Actually, right now I'm working on a scene in which I'm playing a wife-beating racecar driver who leaves his wife after he commits several infidelities. I can assure you that I'm not drawing from my real life for this character. I'm making it up.

That skill of playing make-'em-ups is available to anyone, not just actors. We have the ability to be anything we want in any given moment. We practiced this skill plenty in childhood, while playing make-believe.

Many of us, myself included, carried this skill into middle school and high school, where we were somewhat of a chameleon depending on who we were around at the time. We would heighten certain likes and dislikes of ours and downplay others in order to fit into the crowd. If I'm honest, sometimes I still find myself doing that.

To some degree or another I'm always acting when I'm in public, being some character, turning up some part of myself and turning down others.

Is this surprising to you, off-putting?

I would encourage you to evaluate one of the last interactions you've had. Were you completely yourself? Would there be a way to know if you were? Are you the same person with your friends as you are, say, with your significant other when you're alone?

Consider that who you are, your way of being, is something that you have the ability to mold when needed—like when I was a kid and used the F-word in every sentence and sometimes even in-between words but could keep it totally clean when in the presence of my friends' parents.

This possibility of being something different in any given moment is actually really great news and has the potential to be leveraged in a way that opens up tons of possibility for both ourselves and others. It's not inauthentic, because we are truly so many different things simultaneously and can choose to lean into one way of being instead of another at any given moment in a way that serves others and serves our wider visions.

As I thought about the question of *being* that my coach had asked me, I began to come up with a couple ways of being that would be more resourceful for me than my current state of being was. My state of being at the time clearly wasn't getting me the results I wanted.

One simple *way of being* that I changed was choosing

not to be so concerned about whether I was "bugging" someone if I wanted to make a request of them. Another *way of being* shift was choosing to suspend the beliefs and the limiting voices telling me that nobody would want to work with me on the film project ideas that I had, that they would be too busy, that they would have to be paid, and so on. These changes were choices of who I wanted to be when I approached each phase of the project.

These may seem like small shifts, but the ramifications for me were radical. When I considered the thought that maybe I'm not bothering people and that they might actually love to hear from me and be excited to work with me, it changed how many people I reached out to and how enthusiastic I was in conversation with them.

Now I wasn't necessarily saying I would commit to this new way of being all the time. I was merely willing to try on this new way of being, like a coat, for a few minutes at a time when needed. If I needed a cameraperson or an actor, let's say, I would choose that way of being for that phone call or that request.

So let's take this idea of *being* a step further and peel off one more layer.

There is a distinction here between *being* and *doing*. It was my *thinking* and my *beliefs* (both of which make up my *being*) about myself and the world around me that were rendering my actions (my *doing*) virtually worthless and getting me the same results over and over again. So I could keep working harder and harder and doing more and more, but all that this would produce for me is a greater level of breakdown, stress, anxiety, and fatigue—not a different result.

It was a redesigning of my thoughts and beliefs (my *being*) that needed to be addressed so that the quality of my actions would shift. The way I approached the action and how my being showed up would prove to radically change the results I got.

This continues to be true for me, but only when I choose this New Dreamer principle of paying attention to my *being*. I don't always choose to do so; I don't often, even. More times than not I allow my fears and insecurities to shape my way of being. But I notice that the more I apply this concept, the more habitual it can become. What doesn't work, though, is trying harder without a shift in my way of being.

You see, our belief systems and thoughts, which are revealed in the words we use, are like a GPS system that keeps getting us to the same place over and over again. So trying to increase the speed or effort or time doesn't change the results. It's the GPS system itself that needs to be reprogrammed. It's our framework, the context in which we see ourselves and the world around us, that is getting us the same results time and time again. Creating a new plan and working harder are not necessarily going to help because they are still functioning under a GPS system that we've programmed to achieve the results we're currently getting.

One of the primary purposes of this book is to give simple, practical New Dreamer tools that will help you reprogram your GPS system, so to speak, so that you're *being* shows up differently, which will in turn alter the results you're getting and break you out of any unwanted cyclical patterns you may be experiencing.

The New Dreamer way is to choose to let go of, and question, the beliefs we hold dear, the "truths" that we convince ourselves are "just the way it is." Was it true that I would be bugging someone if I invited them to work alongside me on a particular film project, or that people wouldn't want to work with me, or that they were too busy?

Well, I didn't know because I had never actually tested out this "truth" to see if it was legitimate. I had allowed my resolve, my fixed worldview, to keep me from moving in that direction. I was content to live in my complaints or change my strategy without understanding that I needed a framework shift.

When I decided to suspend that belief and get busy recruiting, I found that I was dead wrong. In fact, I found that people in Los Angeles were very excited to be part of a project that would actually be followed through to completion. And within six months I had about thirty-five volunteers on set with me in a huge warehouse in downtown L.A., filming an action script I had written, produced, and was acting in.

My quality and direction of action changed when I changed my way of being and my made-up beliefs—the thinking that had kept me stuck for nearly a decade.

What are some other ways of being that New Dreamers use?

During a sales conversation I can choose to *be* the type of person that doesn't mind rejection. During a coaching conversation I can choose to *be* a person who is bold and fearless, telling my client exactly what I think without pulling punches. Before I walk on a movie set or into a business meeting I can choose to *be* a guy who believes that he can do a great job in that particular role. When I'm at home I can choose to be a husband who serves his wife.

I can be, and often am, the opposite of these things. But you and me have the option and opportunity to commit to a different way of being intentionally. We don't have to maintain this way of being at all times; I'm not even sure that's realistic. But it's something that we can commit to being for a few minutes or an hour at a time in order to serve the purpose of fulfilling our wider visions and getting the results that we want.

Who would you need to *be* in order to tackle the next big challenge in bringing your dream to fruition?

7

The Truth About You

*"It's never too late
to have a happy childhood."*
~TOM ROBBINS

Author Tom Robbins says that it's never too late to have a happy childhood. I love this because it's not only a little shocking, and seemingly untrue at first, but it also illustrates an important point about perspective and focus. Human beings have an amazing ability to create their realities—how life occurs to them in the moment—by choosing what to focus on, what to remember, and what to rehearse. While this can be applied to just about any circumstance, we'll first look at this example of childhood.

When I think back to my childhood there are probably ten—maybe twenty—memories that I rehearse often. These are the ones that I would consider to be "my childhood," even though there are a million potential memories available to define that period of my life. So my childhood occurs to me a certain way—bad, good, hard, scary, fun, or whatever—depending on this handful of memories that I contemplate most often.

For example, I could think about how my family moved eleven times before my eleventh birthday and how tough it was to constantly leave friends just when friendships were being established. Then I can meditate on how we were financially destitute at times, and how my three brothers, my mom, my dad, and I had to live with relatives for months at a time. I could think about how we were packed into a tiny apartment in a low-income area, or how I had to move out of the house before I even graduated high school because my mom could no longer afford to raise four boys on her own after my parents divorced.

Now that's not a tragic childhood, by any means, but it paints a pretty bleak picture, one that carries certain thoughts and feelings along with it. Most of these feelings come from a victim mindset—not a very resourceful place to be if I want to be productive and effective in the pursuit of my dreams.

Okay, now let's look at another option. What happens when I begin to think about how my parents bought me a guitar early in my life and constantly encouraged me to follow my dreams, or how my dad and I would pull out our guitars and the Beatles' complete songbook and play songs for hours, working out harmonies and having a blast?

I could also remember how my mom worked two or three jobs at a time after the divorce, to make sure that we always lived in a decent house and neighborhood, always ate well, and were clothed in cool, trendy clothes to avoid being shamed at school.

I could think about how my parents instilled in me the value of hard work and an entrepreneurial spirit that led my older brother and me to start a profitable indoor plant business, called "The Plant Guys," when I was eighteen and he was nineteen.

These thoughts and memories create a totally different feeling inside of me and cause my childhood to occur to me differently. These thoughts make me feel like I could take life by the horns and accomplish whatever I set my mind to do.

What if you were to come up with ten to twenty great childhood memories and write them down in detail, and then you began telling those stories over and over to your friends, family, and significant other? How differently might your childhood appear to you?

So that's a simple example of how to apply this principle of focus, memories, and rehearsal to the past and alter the way things occur to you in the present. This principle also naturally applies to the process of getting the things that we want in the future.

Just like the thoughts about my childhood I focus on cause my childhood experience to occur to me in a certain way, the way I perceive myself affects every interaction I have with another human being and every task I take on throughout the day.

For example, if you're getting ready to sing in front of some people, audition for a part in a TV show, or meet a prospective client for a business endeavor, the way you see yourself is going to radically affect the way you come across in that room or at that meeting. The way you show up, your way of being, will largely depend on what you choose to focus on beforehand.

That's why I have a couple different lists in the notes section of my phone that I go over just before meeting with a coaching client or stepping into the audition room or speaking to a group of people. One of the lists is called "The Truth About You." In this list I have encouraging quotes about me from people I respect or clients I've had. These quotes talk about the effect I've had in their lives and how they view me. They remind me of who I am. They serve as a reminder of the "me" that I sometimes (often) forget when I give my inner critic center stage in my thoughts.

The other list I have is called "Big Wins." This is a list of big things, in my estimation, that I have objectively and undeniably accomplished. And when I rehearse and focus on these things and choose to remember them, I begin to see myself differently.

These lists aren't just a positive thinking exercise that I use to replace my negative thoughts. While this may be partially and temporarily helpful, there is a deeper truth at work here. The things on this list are more authentic examples of who I am and what I'm capable of doing when my perception isn't clouded by my insecurities, fears, and desire to please others. I'm not focusing on the flukes of who I was or what I did. The flukes represent the small "me" that chooses safety over progress, playing small rather than going after what I really want. That's not the authentic expression of who I am; the lists are. These lists actually constitute a re-centering of the real "me," the "me" that is capable of great things. And this isn't just true of me, but of you, too.

This New Dreamer mindset regarding how we occur to ourselves has a radical effect on our performances of a task or song or interaction with another person. It greatly increases our chances of getting the results we want in life—relationally, financially, and in terms of achieving our goals. Rehearsing these big wins allows us to lock onto a memory that is going to be more resourceful for us, one that is going to serve us better when it comes to realizing our visions.

The other option is to absorb the last piece of bad news we just heard, foster some resentment, or internalize a limiting voice about ourselves, and take that into the next situation. When we do this, we come across as much more tentative, which reduces our power. The way we come across, that is, the way we're *being* if we choose this path, is going to be much different.

This New Dreamer idea is a small, intentional shift of

mind but it has the potential to make a massive difference in how you approach your life, especially the parts of it that scare you. And as we approach life differently, we begin to get different results.

So what is true about you? A lot of things are true about you, but what is going to be the most resourceful truth about you that you can rehearse before stepping into the next call, audition, meeting, or task?

It's never too late to have a happy childhood, and it's never too late to change your thinking in a way that will change your life.

Are you willing to write down your "The Truth About You" list now? What are some things that people have said about you recently or even in the past that have been meaningful to you—things that really connected with you in a way that had a big impact and encouraged you? Are you willing to write those things down? Once you start your list, you may become more aware of these statements and subsequently capture and add them to the list as you encounter them.

Usually the statements that are the most powerful for me are the ones that come from people I respect who are in line with the particular goals that I'm currently after.

Now, notice what goes through your mind as you begin to think about these "The Truth About You" statements. If you're not able to think of many, or any, notice your thoughts as they come up. For me, if I allow my insecure self to have center stage, I can slip into thoughts like, "Well, she doesn't *really* know me, and if she did she wouldn't think that," or, "Oh, he was just being nice." Allow yourself to let go of those thoughts as you write down the statements. Choose to believe that these people have the right to their own opinions and that they are being genuine when saying these things to you.

Even if you doubt their sincerity (notice if this is a pattern for every person and every compliment), it's more resourceful to believe that it might actually be true. That belief will lead to greater possibility.

Start your "Big Wins" list today. Think through the accomplishments that you're proud of, and jot them down on a separate list. This isn't a time to be humble and downplay what you've done. You can simply jot down the objective facts of what you have achieved, so you can look back and see who you are and what you're capable of when you're being your most authentic self—your most heroic *you.*

8

Half Full

"Pessimism leads to weakness,
optimism to power."
~WILLIAM JAMES

Some time ago I asked my wife if she considered me to be an optimist or a pessimist. Without hesitation she said, "A pessimist." You see, I'm a recovering pessimist. And while it came as a bit of a shock to me to hear her feedback, it wasn't devastating because I knew I didn't have to stay stuck in the mindset of pessimism.

I, like you, have other options.

Dr. Martin Seligman, who is considered the foremost expert on the *function* of optimism and pessimism, came to two primary conclusions as a result of more than a thousand studies over a twenty-year period with over half a million children and adults. Let's talk about the first conclusion and then address the second later in the chapter.

The first conclusion is that optimism makes us much more effective, as it relates to accomplishing our goals and dreams. Optimists—and New Dreamers, since New Dreamers are optimists—are higher achievers than pessimists; they achieve more at school, on the job, and on the playing field, while pessimists perform at a far lower level, even though the pessimists may have equal or greater talent than optimists.

Optimists (and New Dreamers) also have better health than pessimists and suffer from depression far less than pessimists do. The effectiveness of the New Dreamer comes as a result of how they interact with three primary areas of limiting voices about life's circumstances.

The first is how permanent a situation seems to be. The New Dreamer can bounce back much more easily from failure, or some perceived negative event, than the pessimist can because the New Dreamer sees the situation as temporary, in line with the medieval Persian quotation, "This too shall pass." This allows the New Dreamer to get back on the path toward their goals and success much faster and much more often.

The pessimist will not only imagine a tough or uncomfortable situation to be permanent but will also look for permanent sources for the circumstance—reasons why these failures continue over and over again, even if this particular manifestation of it goes away. The New Dreamer simply sees failure as a temporary setback in a world that is otherwise filled with opportunity and possibility and will even specifically point to a transient cause for the unwanted situation and then get right back on track and back into the game.

For example, when the New Dreamer's bank account is low, she might think, "I had some big expenses come up these past couple of months out of the blue. I sure am glad I had the resources to cover them, and I'm looking forward to the fruition of this new business opportunity into which I've been investing my time." On the other hand, the pessimist might think, "I'm not qualified for a different job, so I'm pretty much stuck with this income level."

Another reason the New Dreamer is more effective is because she sees a certain universal, pervasive quality to good events. For instance, when she gets a raise at work, she allows the joy of this good fortune to bleed into every area of her life and affect it as a whole. The pessimist does the same thing, but the other way around. When the pessimist, for instance, gets a parking ticket, she has a difficult time compartmentalizing this misfortune and says to herself, "This is a microcosm of my entire life; everything is falling apart." One failure in one area of the pessimist's life is equivalent to being a failure in every aspect. On the other hand, when the New Dreamer gets a ticket she might say, "Well, good thing I got that raise today. It'll cover that and then some." Not allowing the ticket to pull her into a low mood and into a downward spiral of negative thoughts, the New Dreamer stays on the path toward success and focused on the next small action she needs to take in order to bring her goals closer to completion and her dream nearer to realization.

New Dreamers also tend not to personalize a negative event and instead look to outside sources and causes, whereas the pessimist will internalize a bad outcome and blame herself, thinking that she is the source and saying, "This kind of thing always happens to me. There must be something wrong with me." For this reason, New Dreamers also tend to be much more confident than pessimists. When something great happens, a New Dreamer sees herself as the cause, the one who created the positive circumstances. Therefore, she sees much more possibility in the future, since she's the creator of the positive events in her life, and when we step into the driver's seat of our lives, we're always more effective at attaining superior results.

Okay, so if it's true that pessimists are more depressed, less healthy, and achieve less than optimists, why is pessimism so much more common than optimism? Why isn't everybody an optimist just simply as a result of trial and error?

A pessimistic outlook has certain immediate payoffs, one in particular being emotional preparation. When we say to ourselves (about an upcoming audition, singing performance, interview, or meeting), "I don't think this is going to work out," or, "I don't feel like this is going to go well or lead anywhere," or, "I don't really care if this comes through or not," it softens the blow of disappointment if the opportunity doesn't pan out.

I caught myself doing this very thing just a few days ago on my way to see a potential coaching client. I had my list of reasons why this wasn't going to go well or work out favorably, such as, "He's accomplished so much and is older and super educated and is already making a big impact on the world. What is little old me going to have to offer him that he doesn't already know? This is pointless, a waste of time."

After I let that roll for a few seconds my defense mechanism automatically kicked in, and I started thinking, "Well, it's totally fine if it doesn't work out because I have other things going on in which I would like to focus my attention, like finishing my book, so it might actually be better if it doesn't work out. Besides, if I did sign with the client, I'm not even sure if I'll be able to provide the value needed week to week, and he'll see that I'm not up for the task, and I'll be mortified."

You can see the downward spiral of my thinking as it continued. It's a mechanism that helps us emotionally prepare for failure because we don't think we'll be able to handle the full force of disappointment that could come our way if we really want something, believe that it's possible to attain, and then don't get it.

The truth is, it sort of works. It does have a way of curbing some of the sting of the little disappointments throughout the day. It gives us some perceived power by slightly disconnecting us from our desires.

But the problem is that when we choose to rehearse a

pessimistic outlook, in which we don't believe in the possibility of great things, our whole lives become disappointments. Yes, we partially guard ourselves from the small disappointments of our daily lives, but we live in an altogether safe, boring, and disappointing world. We walk around with a black cloud over our heads, with the poisoned perspective of pessimism, and fail to see or take advantage of the opportunities that are right in front of our faces. We then become far less effective at reaching our goals.

I feel the pain of these words as I write them, not just because it's what my world looked like for over a decade, which it most certainly did, but because it's what I still catch myself slipping into daily. I've rehearsed this pessimistic way of thinking so much that it comes pretty naturally.

Just yesterday I got a call from the car dealership service department saying that after three days and a full diagnostic they couldn't get my car to repeat the problem I brought it in to get repaired—the seatbelt light was coming on and chiming even though the seatbelt was buckled. My wife said to me, "That's great, you got to drive around a new luxury rental car for free for three days."

That was not at all where my head was.

No, I was thinking, "What a colossal waste of time this was, and we all know that the problem is going to repeat itself when I get the car back, and I'm going to have to waste another couple days bringing it back to the dealer, getting a rental car again..." and so on and so on. While I've made some headway replacing this habit with the New Dreamer habit of optimism, I've obviously still got some serious ground to cover.

Now, very few people would come right out and admit that they are pessimists. I certainly wouldn't want to, even though pessimism is clearly a habit that I'm still in the process of replacing. No, we have different language that we use to describe ourselves in kinder terms, don't we? We say things like, "I'm a realist." The so-called realist (a euphemism for pessimist) might say things like, "Get your head out of the clouds," or, "Get real." The problem here is that pessimistic thinking is the furthest thing from reality. Being realistic is being open to possibility. In fact, another way of thinking of, or even defining, optimism is "possibility thinking." The New Dreamer thinks in the context of possibility instead of scarcity; scarcity is the mindset that only sees, and fixates on, what is not possible.

A pessimistic person is not only blind to *existing* opportunities but also shuts down *potential* opportunities, too. Many people tend to think that having a nay-saying attitude is more intelligent, or more in touch with the way the world really is. Dr. Seligman, in light of his findings about pessimists doing worse in just about every measurable area of life than optimists, says, "Holding a pessimistic theory of the world may be the mark of sophistication but it is a costly one." Keeping a pessimistic view of the world costs us our joy, our effectiveness, and our ability to recognize and create opportunity, and could ultimately cost us our key relationships and dreams.

But there's really good news. The second overall conclusion, and by far the most shocking to the psychological and medical communities, was that optimism could be learned. It's not like pessimism is a permanent personality trait. If we practice it enough it begins to look like it's our set personality, but the truth is that it's just a habit; it's simply something that we practice repeatedly until it becomes a program that we naturally start to rehearse, and consequently achieve the associated results...or lack of results.

We can, through intentional repetition, reprogram optimism back into our outlooks. Optimism is simply a language—a language that the New Dreamer uses to her advantage. When we program out the pessimistic thoughts by reprogramming optimistic language, we begin to change the way things occur to us, which in turn changes our performance and actions, which, of course, changes the results that we get in life.

So instead of being stuck in the pessimistic mindset of what *is* and what *was* and thinking that the present and past demonstrate the way things will always be (aka our default future), we use future-based language to create a different future.

Through future-based, generative language we create different possibilities, declaring that we are committed to accomplishing certain goals and then watching as they come to fruition. Because we live into the future we see coming toward us. That future can be the default future (the one that is bound to occur if nothing shifts in us), or it can be the new, declared future that we're committed to living into.

Since optimism is a combination of language, programming, and habit, it's misleading to use the words "optimist" and "pessimist" to describe individuals, since it gives the feeling of permanence, as if we were somehow born as one or the other. Since these dispositions are learned and fortified through practice, it's good to think of yourself somewhere on a *continuum* between pessimism and optimism, based on your past and present habits. Have you repeated a pessimistic viewpoint enough lately that you are currently more on that side of the continuum? We have the ability to move toward the opposite side of the continuum through repetition, through noticing and choosing what language we use—both the language of our thoughts and our words.

The same is true when it comes to being born a "good singer" or with "natural talent." There really is no such thing. Singing well comes from proper technique and, more importantly, building up the muscles in your vocal tract through exercise and repetition. Similarly, optimism is like a muscle that is built up through exercise and repetition. Both optimism and singing are learned habits that, through repetition, produce particular results.

One specific optimistic exercise and declaration that I

rehearse often is, "I'm a living example of a thankful person who always quickly recovers from setbacks no matter how difficult or frequent they are." This certainly isn't true for me all the time, but it is who I am when I'm on top of my game. I know that this is possible for me, and the more aware of it and committed to it I am, the more it will begin to look as if it is actually my permanent personality—even though there is really no such thing as permanent personality.

Let's look at some habits, practices, and characteristics of New Dreamers. I always find that distinctions like optimism (the New Dreamer mindset) vs. pessimism and very specific descriptions of the thoughts and behaviors of each help me and my clients see exactly where we are in any given moment and be able to shift our thoughts and behaviors accordingly.

New Dreamers regularly interrupt negative trains of thought. Like the example above in which I was driving to meet with a potential client, the negative train of thought often begins with a "logical" reason why this meeting or audition or performance or project probably will not go well. And this begins to spiral into a deeper level of automatic defense mechanisms, which brings down my mood, confidence, and vitality.

Now, there may be some truth to the logical reasons that we've come up with as an argument that this endeavor will not work out. It's understandable that we would think these negative thoughts. But it's not resourceful when it comes to achieving our goals. As Voltaire says, "The most important decision you make is to be in a good mood." Since our emotional states are connected to our thoughts, and we have power over what we think, we have control over our moods. And while this negative train of thought may be understandable and not completely far-fetched, it's not going to help our moods, which create our ways of being in the moment. It will shut down possibilities and not allow us to get the things we want in life, even though we're more than capable of attaining them.

So, let's go back to the rest of the story, when I was on my way to meet that client. After a minute or so, I noticed that my thoughts were beginning to get into this downward spiral of negative trains of thought. That was the first step toward getting something different—noticing what was happening when listening to the limiting voices. In the past I may have continued those thoughts for hours or days, even. Once I noticed them, I didn't beat myself up about it, because I didn't have the time or the desire to jump into a shame spiral. Instead I had compassion with myself and said, "Yes, it's understandable that I would think these thoughts, and there may even be a shred of truth in them, but for now, I want to succeed; for now, I want to be in a good mood; for now, I want to walk with confidence and with a way of being that is going to be the most resourceful for getting what I want and serving the world powerfully, starting with this one person I'm about to meet."

Recognizing and interrupting these trains of thought

is important because they can quickly begin to distort our understanding and negatively affect the way a circumstance is occurring to us, and this blocks our ability to see possibility and find solutions to setbacks and perceived roadblocks.

Once I had interrupted the negative thought pattern that had begun to take on a life of its own, I started thinking about what might be possible. I thought, "This could lead to a real breakthrough for both this person and also for me. He could have a real willingness and openness to creating the type of relationship with me that would cause a major shift in his life. I could be a part of helping him change culture because of the influence he already has." As I started thinking these things, which were more full of truth and possibility, it began to infuse me with a sense of excitement and anticipation. I began to settle into the fact that it probably would happen.

And the final step for me was getting clear about the idea that working with this client was something I wanted to do and that I would follow through with the work if given the chance. This is something I realized that I hadn't actually done. I had been too busy thinking it wouldn't happen to settle into the reality that it had a strong possibility of occurring. This final thought grounded me in a new way. It became real for me in that moment.

Another trait of the New Dreamer is that he is seldom surprised by trouble. The very first line of author and psychiatrist, M. Scott Peck's book, *The Road Less Traveled*, is,

"Life is difficult." He goes on to say that once we understand this, life gets easier because our expectations of what *should* be begin to shift.

This is the perspective of the New Dreamer. Now, the New Dreamer doesn't want trouble and calamity in his life, of course—but he also doesn't live inside the limiting idea that the sky is falling and doom is imminent. He understands that everybody encounters hardships in their lives, and when a challenge presents itself, he interrupts the negative trains of thought, such as, "Why does this always happen to me," or, "My life is cursed," and then says, "Okay, what can I *do* to solve this?" or, "How might the solution to this problem lead to a breakthrough for me or those around me?" or, "In light of this, what would I like to create?"

The New Dreamer also looks for partial solutions to problems. She understands that rarely do we have one hundred percent (or even fifty percent, for that matter) of the information to take action toward at least a partial resolution of a problem. Instead of getting stuck in a state of analysis paralysis, she says to herself, "Well I don't know how to get from A to Z yet, but I think I have an idea of how to get from A to C, and from there I trust I'll find a way to D and so on until we tackle the entire problem." This type of thinking allows the optimist to avoid the stuck place of needing things to be perfect before getting into action—instead believing that the insights will come once she's in action.

Three-time Emmy nominated film and Broadway

director, Robert Allan Ackerman, said that he doesn't worry about knowing what to do or having the creative insights before the shooting or editing of a film; instead, he trusts that ideas will come along the way as he engages in the process of making the film, "Because they always do," he says. Mr. Ackerman is a New Dreamer.

Where do you fall on the continuum between optimism and pessimism? Which way of thinking have you gotten into the habit of rehearsing so that it now feels like your personality? What small shift can you choose to make in your life today that would push you closer to the optimistic mindset?

Write down one non-resourceful thought or belief that you've been entertaining that you're now committed to interrupt and challenge. Is there an attribute of optimists that you notice you're not currently practicing? Are you willing to intentionally implement that attribute into your life this week?

One final thought is that it's possible to feel discouraged or feel like a failure because we can't control the thoughts that come into our head. It's important to remember that we can't choose which thoughts pass through our mind— nobody can—but we can decide which ones we dwell on and assign significance to in each moment. This is where we have the power over our thoughts, and this is the epicenter of the choice between optimism and pessimism.

Pessimism makes us weaker and less effective in just about every area in our lives, and optimism does the opposite. Let's choose power and productivity, make true contributions to those around us, and be of service to the world. This will take us further along the path toward peace, purpose, wealth, and success.

Optimism isn't a feeling or a personality type; it's a tool, a tool that New Dreamers choose to use whether they feel like it or not. And it's a very useful tool as it relates to being motivated, being in good spirits, and accomplishing our goals.

I did end up signing that client and still work with him; it's been a really fun journey. There is so much more possible for you and for me when we interrupt our limiting voices and live into a way of thinking that opens up a greater degree of possibility.

PART 3

RACKETEERING

9

What a Racket

*"Every complaint is a little story
the mind makes up that
you completely believe in."*
~Eckhart Tolle

Rackets are stories that we make up about ourselves, others, or the world around us that are in competition with what we say we really want in life. They are belief systems, built on lies, that we tell ourselves about how we are helpless and weak, particularly when we come face-to-face with opportunities and challenges.

Having an awareness of these rackets, and choosing to take responsibility for them, is one of the most powerful of all New Dreamer tools we can use to alter our performance, our actions, and subsequently our results in life.

The idea of a racket conjures up images of the 1920's when a seemingly legitimate business, a restaurant for example, has an entire back room where there are illicit operations going on, like prostitution, gambling, alcohol smuggling, and so on.

This is a perfect image of what it looks like when we run a racket on ourselves. Our racket begins with a negative thought or complaint that seems perfectly legitimate, but there are all sorts of illicit motivations and consequences going on in the background—motivations of which we are usually unaware.

Before we jump into an example I want to acknowledge that some complaints or negative outlooks—and the potential feelings of hopelessness associated with them—can be accompanied by a lot of pain and often some very legitimate grievances. I don't want to invalidate that or pretend those feelings don't exist. Rather, I want to open up a potentially greater awareness of the behind-the-scenes action associated with it and the power of change that is possible once the racket is more fully exposed. So, let's walk through the four steps of a racket together.

Step 1: The Complaint (Limiting Voice)

The very expression of a complaint is a declaration that you are in a powerless victim state, whereas understanding the hidden, unarticulated areas of the racket allows us the opportunity to take a measure of ownership and jump back into the driver's seats of our lives.

One of my personal favorite rackets, and a common one for many of my clients, is the complaint, "It's nearly impossible to break into that industry." This is a preferred racket for artists and creative entrepreneurs. For entrepreneurs the face of it may change slightly to look something like, "That industry is already over-saturated," or something similar. But it's really the same complaint and underlying belief.

A complaint is a pretty good indicator that a racket is present. It is a declaration of powerlessness. It assumes the power is *out there* and not inside of me, which of course is not true. And this kind of statement—and there are hundreds of examples like these—has some kind of feeling attached to it, that is, some kind of associated behavior or attitude.

Step 2: How We React When We Believe the Limiting Voice is True

I know for me, when I entertain this thought, it produces a feeling of fatigue or of being overwhelmed; it shuts me down and demotivates me, keeping me out of action. My mood plummets, and I'm tempted to look for some kind of distraction like television or social media or food (ice cream, probably), through which I'm either seeking escape or validation or comfort.

Since we never do anything that we're not getting something out of, why would we entertain this complaint, given what it produces in us? Why would we choose to tranquilize ourselves so that we're trudging through a swamp of molasses while trying to reach our goals in life?

This is where we begin to get into that illicit, hidden operation that is going on in the background—an operation of which we're often unaware.

Step 3: The Payoff for Believing the Limiting Voice is True

Well, here's why I choose to entertain this illicit operation, when I do. It allows me to have a good excuse to play small, stay safe, and never have to actually do the hard work of testing the truth of whether it's impossible to break into the industry. As long as I believe it's virtually impossible, then my lack of risk-taking begins to feel to me like a prudent decision.

I may think to myself, "Why waste my time pursuing a dead end when I could just get a job at a company and be 'guaranteed' to work my way up, as long as I stick with it? At least there's a clear-cut path there, unlike a career as a singer."

What are some other reasons I might entertain this racket? I wouldn't have to fail, or more importantly, look like a failure in front of others. I wouldn't have to do the hard work it takes to create a start-up business or achieve a certain level of mastery as an actor.

This is enough to illustrate the point, but there could potentially be a dozen more reasons with a little further exploration. I had no idea all this was happening. Being aware of it helped me to realize that I am *choosing* to believe this complaint, this limiting thought, and this worldview. I'm choosing it because I'm getting a lot out of believing it. To some degree I'm self-sabotaging my own deeper desires without even realizing what I'm doing, in favor of a false sense of comfort in the moment.

So, when we do choose to buy into our rackets—and we've all got 'em—what are we giving up that might otherwise be possible for us?

Step 4: The Cost of Believing the Limiting Voice is True

I gave up pursuing a career as an actor for about a decade. I gave up a certain amount of my vitality, my life, and my passion. I still had my singing, and my businesses, but there was a nagging sense in me that there was another more deeply seated desire that I was avoiding. That thought (and associated feeling) took up a certain amount of bandwidth in my mind and lent itself to shame (another racket), which carried with it a level of depression and despair. I was giving up some happiness by surrendering a sense of confidence that I was the type of person that conquers obstacles and moves fearlessly toward his dreams. I was giving up being an inspiration to others who were too afraid to pursue their dreams.

New Dreamers understand that the victim mindset—evidence that we're being run by one of our rackets—is the default position of the brain. Like weeds in your yard, you don't have to plant these thoughts in your mind; they work themselves in there if left unattended for a while. And like weeds, rackets masquerade themselves as something valuable. The weed looks as though it may be a flower or a vegetable, but the truth is that it will eventually take over and kill every other living thing in the garden if it's not identified and dealt with for what it really is.

There is nothing *wrong* with you because you have these rackets. This is the path of least resistance. This is the current that sweeps us up if we don't intentionally choose another path. We can choose a different path at any moment; that's the good news. We don't need a year to heal from this derailed path that we've been choosing. That's another racket, another limiting voice. We can choose a different path in any moment. We can begin moving toward a new commitment and a new path right now. That's the beauty in the power of choice.

So, what complaints do you have that might be holding you back from moving toward the thing that you really, really want? Are you willing to interrogate the truth of your belief about how "nearly impossible" it is to attain that goal?

One of the main things I do now as a success coach is help people uncover and redesign their thoughts and beliefs that constitute rackets. That's what my coach did, and still does, for me. I highly recommend finding a good coach or a friend who could help you do an honest inventory of the beliefs you hold that keep you stuck.

There is a game that I used to play in improv class in which the teacher would wait for the student to make some character choice in a scene and then say, "New choice!" and let the audience see a different option. And after a few moves with that new character choice the teacher would say it again and again and again. It was a fun way of seeing that there are many different options that an actor and improviser can make quickly and change the outcome of the situation.

If you are making choices that allow you to believe lies that are holding you back in life, I challenge you now to make a *new choice*.

10

I've Been Here Before

"Creativity involves breaking out
of established patterns
in order to look at things in a different way."
~Edward de Bono

When I first decided to get help and begin on the track of transformation with my own coach, it was because I started noticing a disconcerting pattern in my life that I was no longer interested in repeating. I had been pursuing music as a singer-songwriter and guitar player and found that just as I was on the cusp of accomplishing a major goal, everything would seem to fall apart, and the opportunity would be lost. This happened over and over again, and I began to realize that it wasn't likely that this was "just the way things were," as I had been telling myself for so long, but that I was somehow complicit in causing the same outcome to reoccur.

At first when I noticed this pattern, I saw it as a problem that needed to be fixed. I figured there was something wrong or deficient within me. I thought that I must have missed out on something in my childhood.

But there wasn't anything wrong with me, just like there isn't anything wrong with you. The very idea that I was broken and needed to be fixed was a racket keeping me stuck and out of action until I had some elusive piece of information or experience that would make me whole— as if that piece would get me back into action, on the path toward my life's goals. Maybe I could go through a bunch of years of psychotherapy or read enough books or live in a monastery for a year. I didn't know what to do.

But the simple truth is that I had adopted a way of thinking and a way of being that was the perfect system for the result I was getting. I had chosen a set of beliefs that produced actions that continued to yield a particular outcome. It became cyclical because I was viewing it as a problem within my current framework rather than looking to shift the framework itself. The so-called "problem" was perfectly aligned with the encasing worldview that I carried around with me, the lens through which I saw everything in life. So working on the "problem" was a meaningless pursuit because the system of belief I was adhering to was perfectly engineered to produce the same unsatisfying results.

No matter how much effort I spent trying to fix it, my life wouldn't change until the framework itself changed.

Focusing on life's "problems" causes them not only to grow—since what we give attention to we begin to find more evidence for—but it also makes the symptom the focal point rather than seeking to highlight the root cause.

I remember as a kid asking my mom the question, "Is this medicine going to help me to *get* better or just help me to temporarily *feel* better?" I was far less interested in treating symptoms; I wanted to strike at the root of the issue and solve it for good, not simply put a bandage on it.

The coaching work that I do now, both being coached and coaching others, is a continuation of my childhood disdain for the hyper focus on the symptoms rather than the system—on evidence rather than origin. I am so results-driven that I only want to stay in the world of symptoms for as long as it takes to diagnose the cause and then really dig into what the solution might look like.

Anytime we're not getting the results that we want in our lives, it means that it's simply time to seek out a new system. Our default, when life isn't going our way, is to personalize the problem. This is the path of saying, "There must be something wrong with me." We can skip all that and live from our futures rather than from our pasts. Constantly looking at patterns from the past and projecting them into the future is living one's default future, based on past results.

This is the way that our life starts to look like Bill Murray's character, Phil, from the film *Groundhog Day*, in which he's living the same day, February 2nd, over and over and over again, for about 10 years. This isn't a resourceful way to live and doesn't lead to the new future that is possible for us. How can it, when we're living the same day again and again? We don't have to live that way. There is another option—to change the system. Transforming the systems we live by transforms our lives.

There are two different aspects of systems that govern our lives, and therefore the results we get. The first is your thinking system, that is, your way of seeing yourself and the world around you. The other is your system of doing. This system encompasses the practical, like exercising five mornings a week from nine to ten in order to reach our fitness goals.

Our thinking systems take precedence over our systems of doing, because without a shift in our thinking, our doing can only produce the same types of results it has always produced: results that comprise our default futures, based on our resolved judgments about ourselves and the world around us. Examining and redesigning the systems of our thoughts and beliefs is the beginning of our transformations. This can be done with a coach, with a friend, by reading books, through silent reflection, and more.

As our limiting thoughts and beliefs begin to transform into a bigger view of what is possible, the quality and tenacity of our actions also begin to shift and then so do the results in our lives. This is where the systems of doing come in and begin to become transformative.

One recent example of a system of doing for me is my continued writing of this book. For about a decade my system was to talk about the fact that I wanted to write a book *someday*. And maybe I would complain about not having enough time or not having enough to say. Certainly part of my system was to think, "I just don't have the capacity to pull it off." All of this led to inaction. That was a system of doing, based on my system of thinking. It wasn't a very effective system if my real desire was to have written a book.

So I implemented a new system. I wrote down my self-created due date for completion of the book and put it on the wall next to my desk; I built structures of accountability around me by telling people what I was doing; and I made a goal of writing two pages per day, five days a week. That worked fine for a while, but then I noticed that I wasn't getting my two pages done everyday due to auditions, rehearsals, or, frankly, slipping into the habit of pleasing others instead of working on my own priority of finishing this book within the timeline I had decided on.

So I had the option to choose to personalize my short-comings, which would look like delving into my past and wondering why my parents didn't instill in me the ability to be disciplined and stay on track. And I could talk about how discipline is just not part of my core personality, which would give me a good excuse to get out of action and maybe even jump into the wound-licking place of shame and self-pity.

Or, I could skip all of that nonsense and create a new system. If the system ceases to work, I can choose to personalize it and think it's because there's something wrong with me, or I can simply choose another, more effective system.

I keep a running tally of hash marks on an index card next to my computer of the number of pages written during the given week, and I commit to myself, and to my coach, that I will have ten pages written each week, regardless of whether I write two pages per day or ten pages on any combination of days inside that week. This keeps me locked into my goal for completion while freeing me from the tyranny of feeling behind when I miss one or more of my writing days.

After all, there really is no such thing as being behind, since we make up and choose what goes onto our schedules and what due dates we will adhere to and at what jobs we decide to continue working. The very thought, "I'm behind," is simply a story that we could choose to believe or not. I find that it's more resourceful not to give into it. It's a racket that has the ability to make me anxious, which is not a place that tends to produce the feelings and actions that lead to the accomplishment of my vision. So instead of entertaining that feeling of being behind, and pretending it's real, I can ask myself, "What system can I create that will guarantee the results that I want?" or at least have the greatest chance of doing so.

That's the great thing about systems: they're made up. New Dreamers create or choose new systems whenever they notice one isn't producing the results they want. While many creatives feel like routines and systems stifle creativity, New Dreamers understand that implementing systems is a highly creative act that constructs an environment where creativity can thrive in an intentional and measurable way.

Have you noticed patterns in your life that repeat themselves over and over again? It's not that there is something wrong with you or that you are broken or didn't have the right upbringing to equip you to be successful. What kind of system can you implement now to support your success?

11

It's All Made Up Anyway

*"Man is a make-believe animal:
he is never so truly himself
as when he is acting a part."*
~WILLIAM HAZLITT

I just can't do scary movies anymore.

I'm a full-grown man who is still afraid of the dark, and I attribute that to how many horror films I used to watch as a kid. I was obsessed with them because they would make me *feel*, and I loved that. My heart would pound, my hands would get clammy, and I would genuinely sense that I was in danger.

But there was nothing really to fear. I was sitting safely in my living room on the other side of the television glass, probably eating popcorn. But I was caught up in—and vicariously living through—a story.

In many ways, I haven't stopped doing this. You see, you and I live in a world based on the stories we tell ourselves and vicariously live through. Some of these stories are helpful and spur us on, like, "No matter how bad things are now, there is always a future hope for you." Living through this story will produce certain results. On the other hand, less helpful stories (i.e. limiting voices) might include, "Something terrible is going to happen." Living into this scary story will yield a different sort of result altogether.

Every story we tell about ourselves or about the world around us is built on a network of hidden assumptions that we may or may not realize we hold. While these stories seem very real to us and produce certain associated feelings in us, they are not necessarily real in an objective sense, just like the scary movie isn't reality, even though it *feels* like it is in the moment.

As long as we're suspending disbelief about our made up scary stories, we respond to our fears as if they are real. This makes them real for us and gets us the results associated with our beliefs, whether they're objectively true or not.

One of the most helpful New Dreamer realizations is that all of our stories are made up—all of them. Now, some are certainly based on more objective truth than others, but all of them are made up. If this is true, then we might as well intentionally pick a story that serves our visions rather than one that scares us out of action and into complacency.

One example from my own life is a story that I made up that went something like this: "I'm attempting to pursue acting so late in the game. I should have started sooner, so now I'll never be able to catch up and be a success-ful actor." That story had me scared to death. It still does when I relapse into believing it's objectively true. I chose to replay this scary movie over and over again in my mind for so many years—scaring myself out of action—that it has become a challenging habit to replace.

Notice the shaming "should" language also built into the story—this is always a good indicator that I'm choos-ing a victim position.

What I didn't realize for a very long time was that it was just a story—a made up story. Now, it's a story that is prevalent in society and can be heard from the lips of many of the people in the film industry, but that doesn't take away from the fact that it is only one possible story I can choose to believe—or only one possible movie I can choose to watch.

It's not that it's a really far-fetched belief. If it were, I wouldn't be as tempted to hold onto it. The destructive part of this type of limiting voice is that it not only puts me in low mood and discourages me from moving toward my dreams, but it also shuts down possibility and oppor-tunity. It's very difficult to see a reality that contradicts the way of thinking that we've chosen, so we're more likely to miss opportunities and possibilities that are right in front of our faces.

Since I had made up that story (partially on my own and partially borrowed from others' stories that were vocal-ized to me along the way) and had chosen to believe it, as if it were objectively true, I also had the power to make up a new story—a new framework of meaning to approach life from. I knew that simply trying to put a positive spin on it by attempting to tell myself some motivational cliché when the story presented itself wouldn't work, so I thought about what else might be true.

The truth was that I had accomplished quite a bit since I had decided to really go after acting. In just over a year I had written, produced, and acted in four episodes of a high production web series and a ten-minute action film; I had acquired a manager, and a film, television, and commercial agent; I had acted in a number of other short films; I was auditioning regularly, including a series regular audition for the second season of Fargo; I had booked an LG Electronics commercial (a low-paying, non-union gig but a gig nonetheless); I was spending roughly thirty hours per week doing acting related activities—scene study class, rehearsals, audition technique class, workshops, acting administration (for headshots, résumé, etc.); and was regularly getting feedback on my progress as an actor. As a result I'm becoming more and more proficient as an actor and becoming more employable in the eyes of casting directors.

I was doing all this, yet I was still living in this fatalistic story. So, I chose a new story and wrote it down on an index card and put it on the wall next to my desk. The new story, since it's all made up anyway, says, "I've come so far, and I've only just begun." Since this new story resonated with me as really being true and not simply being a positive spin, it created a new framework of thinking for me.

Another helpful made up story, one that was just as true as any other potential option, was the idea that success is progressively realizing a worthy ideal, as we talked about earlier in this book. If success is simply staying on the path toward my vision, then I was successful as long as I continued to work toward the goals I had set out for myself. In this case that meant continuing to hone the craft of acting with classes, continuing to create my own content to act in, and showing up prepared to my auditions.

Now, this doesn't mean that we can make anything up and cause it to magically materialize, but rather that we can let our thoughts and actions proceed from a new set of chosen stories and watch as our results begin to change.

A new, made up story is a form of declaration that begins to set new possibilities into action, possibilities that may have merely been hidden from our views due to the blinders inherent in the stories from an old way of thinking. We begin to see opportunities that emerge as a result of the new beliefs, thoughts, and actions of the newly invented story.

New Dreamers get that we are all actors maintaining our constructed personalities and our masks (or stories) that we believe to be serving us in life. As William Shakespeare said in his famously quoted monologue from his play, *As You Like It*, "All the world's a stage, and all the men and women merely players." This isn't a condemnation; it's

THE VOICE OF YOUR DREAMS

actually really great news because it reminds us that it's all made up—all of it—and we can choose to write our own story, one that serves us and those around us or to continue to live in the stories that get us the same unwanted results over and over again.

So, how do we discover what stories are dictating our lives? One way is to listen to your judgments and assessments about yourself and the world. Hone in particularly on the ones that have to do with your heart's deepest desires, your true dreams, and your deepest disappointments.

This can sometimes be a challenge to discover on one's own, since we're living inside the framework we've chosen and the stories we've created. Just like we can't see our own eyes without a mirror, I found that working with a coach (a mirror of sorts) was the best way to unearth the stories that had become part of what I thought was reality.

What do you believe? Which made up stories continue to occur to you as "true" or "real," but are keeping you out of action and stuck in your complaints? From which belief systems are you resolved that this is "just the way it is, and nothing can be done to change it?" These so-called problems and roadblocks in your mind reveal the stories that you're living in, and vanish when you develop a new framework of possibility.

One question New Dreamers ask is, "What assumption am I making about this circumstance—which I may be unaware of on the surface—that is giving me this negative outlook?" If you take a second to answer that question, then you can ask yourself another follow up New Dreamer question, "In light of that, what can I make up now, that I haven't already thought of, which would give me a wider selection of choices?"

We're all just acting a part, so which script will serve you and the others around you the most? What can you make up now that will open up a greater degree of opportunity for you?

PART 4

INCREASED PRODUCTIVITY

12

The Commitment Compartment

"There is no abiding success
without commitment."
~TONY ROBBINS

One of the most powerful tools we possess to create the world we want is the ability to commit. We have in us the capacity to dream up a reality, commit ourselves to that made-up future, and have it come to pass. This is one of the most underused New Dreamer principles of success, because most people don't know its effectiveness or feel that they don't have what it takes to exercise it.

The truth is that we exercise this principle all the time without even necessarily realizing it. We put certain things into a place in our hearts and minds, which I call the Commitment Compartment, where we make a decision that something is going to come to pass no matter what.

For example, I'll never walk out of my house naked. I won't do it. I'm absolutely committed to not doing that.

Even if the house were on fire, I would grab the nearest article of clothing and throw it on before heading out the door.

If you have kids, my guess is that you are committed to not letting them go hungry or become homeless. Even if you lost your job and had no opportunities on the horizon, you'd figure it out. Your language about it would reveal a certain resoluteness. If I pressed you on it, you'd say, "I would find a way to feed them. Period." But how do you know? You know because you've placed the determination to feed your kids and give them shelter into your Commitment Compartment.

I can listen to my language or the language of my clients and know whether a particular task or event is in the Commitment Compartment.

Notice the language that you may be using. You might say, "I'm going to pursue being a singer *someday*," or, "I'm *thinking about* building this new app," or, "*Maybe* I'll write a book about that." All of this language is evidence that we don't have any real intentions of pulling the trigger on these ideas.

So how do we change that?

We decide.

It's that simple.

That's not to say that it's easy, but it is that simple. Instead of doing this, often times we live in the land of indecision for days, months, or years.

Anything we want to go into our Commitment Compartment can go there. We have the power to put it there. It's a matter of making a decision and committing to it.

New Dreamers understand that this "all-in" state of putting something into the Commitment Compartment is not a state of being that we need to try to change into, but that it's our natural state; it was our state of being before we began to learn the possibility of not having, being, or doing the things we want.

For most of our lives, we live in this committed state. When we're putting on shoes or showering or going to the grocery store we're committed to getting it done without considering whether we have what it takes to bring it to pass—without really considering the possibility that it might not happen. If a shoelace breaks, we grab a new pair of laces from the drawer and replace them, or we wear a different pair of shoes until we can get to the store for a replacement.

There are an infinite amount of these small tasks and pursuits that effortlessly end up in our Commitment Compartment, but when it comes to the pursuits of our dreams, we often jump out of the committed state. This is most often because of doubt. We jump out of this committed state when we allow doubt to creep into our psyches. Once doubt takes center stage, we shrink back and refrain from taking action. We choose not to move forward. Shakespeare says it best: "Our doubts are traitors and make us lose the good we oft might win by fearing to attempt."

Interestingly enough, doubt is what takes us out of the committed state, and getting into the committed state is the only way to eliminate doubt. Once we get into action and get committed to something, we don't have time to consider doubt. We're too busy moving toward our goals each moment and each day.

This committed state is the state we find ourselves in once we put something into the Commitment Compartment. It's no longer a hope or a dream or a wish but something we have chosen to accomplish no matter what. And the great thing about this state is that it not only eliminates doubt, but also eliminates many of the stuck areas related to doubt that hold us back. We don't consider what to do or how to do it; we simply act—and thus we move forward.

New Dreamers also understand that on the road to success in any endeavor our visions don't change, but our plans change often. It's okay that plans change. That's part of the fun of playing this game called "becoming a great singer" or "starting a new business" or "writing a book." It's perfectly fine that we don't have all the facts and know-how before putting something in the Commitment Compartment and going after it.

Let's use Johnny's story to illustrate the point.

There's a ten-year-old boy named Johnny at a pool party with his family and a bunch of other families when he sees a younger kid, maybe four or five years old, flailing and coughing in the deep end of the pool, not able to tread water. While there are plenty of others around, no one else seems to notice, and it appears to Johnny that time was of the essence for this kid who was close to drowning.

Now, Johnny had never saved anyone from drowning before, didn't know how to, and wasn't the strongest swimmer in the world. In fact, the month prior to this, Johnny had gone out for the junior lifeguard program but failed the basic swimming test in the first round. But Johnny wasn't about to let this kid drown, so he entered the committed state in a hurry and jumped into the water.

Notice that he wasn't in the committed state of being while he was standing at the edge of the pool. It wasn't until he made the decision to toss this drowning kid into his Commitment Compartment that he chose to jump. After he jumped in Johnny realized that he had no strategy for saving this kid. He didn't know *how* to do it, but that didn't matter to him. He was in the committed state and was going to figure it out no matter what. In fact, figuring out how to do it wasn't even a thought. The only thing that existed for him at that moment was a strong desire to succeed in this endeavor.

So Johnny grabbed the kid, but when he did, they both began to sink. Plan A was looking like a failure. Johnny could have been disappointed about his first action not panning out and potentially leading to both of them drowning, but he was in the committed state, so the only option was to successfully get both this kid and himself out of the water alive.

Plan B was to dunk the kid under the water in order to get enough leverage to get himself above water to gulp some air. This was a terrible idea. The kid was now worse off than he was before. So then he dunked himself under the water, and lifted the kid up out of the water so that he could get some air. Johnny repeated this a few frantic times, but this wasn't getting him to his end goal—getting both of them out of the water alive. Plan B was looking like a failure, too. It was time for a new plan—same commitment, same vision, but with a new strategy.

While Johnny couldn't seem to get out of the pattern of dunking the kid and dunking himself to lift the kid, he did notice that if he kicked his legs and feet then he and the kid moved closer and closer to the edge of the pool in the process. So he continued to do that until they reached the side where Johnny gave the kid one last lift to the side of the pool and a couple adults helped pull him out of the water.

Once we place something into the Commitment Compartment—where we say, "I'm going to do whatever it takes to make this thing come to pass"—then the prospects of failure, not knowing how to do something, wondering if we were born with enough talent, and failed plans all begin to fade into the background. None of those stuck places have the kind of power over us that we may have endowed them with in the past.

We know when we're outside of this committed state because the result is inaction.

We wait.

We wait for all kinds of different things. We wait until we know *how*. We wait to see if an endeavor is likely to be successful. We wait until we *feel* like doing something. We wait until our desk is clean. We wait until enough people we trust affirm that it's a good idea. Novelist C.S. Lewis said, "If we let ourselves, we shall always be waiting for some distraction or other to end before we can really get down to our work...seek it while the conditions are still unfavorable. Favorable conditions never come."

New Dreamers put their biggest dreams into the Commitment Compartment, no matter what unfavorable conditions may be present. Once that's taken care of, we spend less time worrying and wondering and hoping, and more time doing what it takes to bring that dream to pass.

What is it that you may be avoiding? What can you place into your Commitment Compartment right now and turn into a project? Think right now about something that you're hoping to do or trying to do or intending to do at some point. Are you willing to shift your thinking about that one thing, to convert it from a "want-to" to a "committed-to"? What might you be putting off that, if you added a greater level of consciousness to it, could possibly transform a far-off dream into something that you can take a small step toward today? Is it possible that you could eventually have enough mastery over it to make a living doing it or use it to enhance the quality of your life or someone else's? Are you willing to place that thing in your Commitment Compartment right now?

13
Stop Stopping

"The most difficult thing is the decision to act,
the rest is merely tenacity. The fears are paper tigers.
You can do anything you decide to do."
~Amelia Earhart

I know very little about algorithms, but I'll never forget the destructive force of Panda. (Panda is a search results ranking algorithm that Google launched in February 2011.) The reason I'll never forget it is because it nearly single-handedly destroyed my Superior Singing Method (SSM) business. It certainly crippled it.

After launching SSM, my business partners and I went to work on the SEO (Search Engine Optimization), which, at the time, was a very laborious and time-consuming process. We understood that nearly every successful endeavor begins with doing a lot of tasks up front that you don't really love doing. So, for months and months and months I wrote article after article that we would spin into many more articles and then link the articles from our site to thousands of other sites, which would create tons of backlinks that made our site look like it got tons of natural traffic.

That's a truncated version of what we did, of course, but after about three to six months of working twenty to thirty hour weeks tackling various aspects of this process, we had ranked about fifteen to twenty keywords to the number one, two, and three spots on Google. This meant that anytime someone typed in a keyword or phrase into a Google search, like "How To Sing" or "How To Improve Your Singing Voice" or "Singing Tips," our site would show up somewhere in the top three spots, mostly in the number one spot.

As you can imagine, we began to get a ton of traffic to the site and to our sales page, which meant a lot more sales and also that I could stop working my two other jobs and just focus on building this new business—until Panda.

When Google released the Panda algorithm, all of our top spots immediately dropped down to page fifteen—not to *spot* fifteen, which would be on the top of page two, but *page* fifteen. I had never before even been to page fifteen on Google, and neither had anybody else, judging by the nearly one hundred percent drop in site traffic and subsequent sales.

I love the Amelia Earhart quotation, "The most difficult thing is the decision to act, the rest is merely tenacity," because this has been true for me in every area in which I have attained some form of measurable success. Somewhere in the space of tension between current reality and the completion of a vision is where most people give up, and, as a result, don't succeed in that particular endeavor. New Dreamers see that the gap between what we want and where we are now in relation to that desire is where tenacity becomes essential. New Dreamers are tenacious.

Bestselling author Rory Vaden has what he calls the *rent axiom*, which says, "Success is never owned. It's rented, and the rent is due everyday."

This is true for any area of life. We know that working out diligently for several weeks and months will afford us the success of being in shape. But the "rent" continues to be due. We can't expect that same level of fitness six months later if we neglect exercise and eat whatever we want.

The same is true for relationships. If we don't invest in our key relationships, the closeness that brings us life begins to drift away.

SSM had a degree of success, but when Panda came around, it was a reminder of this "rent axiom" principle. We couldn't just coast along and expect sustained success without continuing to put work into it. So now we had a choice. We could pack it up and say, "Well, we had a good run," or we could understand that this was only the end if we stopped working on it, or if we stopped paying the rent, so to speak.

I had a sense of this principle at the time, but I felt too devastated and disheartened to even move at first. I couldn't believe it was possible for something like this to happen, to lose all my business and all my income in an instant.

Each limiting voice in my head seemed to shout louder than the next:

- "I always fail."
- "I'll just fail again if I try."
- "I'm stupid."
- "I can't do it."
- "I did it wrong."
- "Nothing's going to work."
- "This is typical of me."
- "I don't deserve success."
- "The 'System' is against me."
- "I'll never have sustained success."

It took me a little while to bounce back from that, for the sole reason that I was listening to, and believing, the limiting voices in my head and allowing them to keep me feeling depressed and hopeless.

After some time we decided to work another angle of driving traffic to our site, and I got busy preparing some of the best content I knew of for twenty-three videos. We filmed all the videos, put them up on YouTube, and within a couple of months they had hundreds of thousands of views, and we began seeing a ton of traffic to our site once again. The YouTube videos were a catalyst that built up our numbers to attract affiliates, which led to much more traffic and many other opportunities and possibilities.

That's a feel-good story that ends well, but the truth is that we're always in process, and the rent continues to require payment. Marketing on the internet changes shape so quickly and so often. We recently took another big hit and are in the process of learning and implementing new marking strategies in order to pay the rent and stay tenacious. Some of the new strategies are working, but many have failed miserably. We still have plenty of ground to cover.

Another important element of tenacity is this New Dreamer principle of investment: The more blood, sweat, and tears you put into an endeavor, the less likely you are to allow it to fail. So, tenacity begets tenacity, and tenacity leads to success.

What are you tempted to give up on right now? What might be right on the other side of some more investment into that project or dream? Are you willing to hold on to that vision and push through the tension for just a little while longer? Is there a vision that you've given up on that you'd be willing to reinvigorate? Take a minute and write about how you can recommit to a dream you have for yourself that you may have given up on some time ago.

14

Pro, Not Perfect

*A lot of people from my generation of music
are so focused on playing things correctly
or to perfection that they're stuck in that safe place."*
~DAVE GROHL (FOO FIGHTERS)

While in graduate school I spent the better part of my final school year working on my master's thesis. I wrote and rewrote it with the help of two of my professors, who gave me continued feedback. They both also told me that the paper had a real possibility of being published in an academic journal, which I had heard was extremely difficult to accomplish.

One of the primary academic journals for which my article was a good fit was called the *Journal of Religion and Health*, whose focus was psychology, spirituality, and medicine. The problem was that the required format for submitting the paper for potential publication was very different from how I had originally formatted it. So, it was going to be a laborious and tedious process to convert it, and I wasn't exactly sure how to do all of the conversions, which seemed like a chore.

So, I began the process of converting it but found that I would avoid working on it for days and weeks at a time. After several months had passed, I was so sick of looking at it on my desk that I finally just packaged up the paper, put it into an envelope—only partially converted over— and sent it to the *Journal of Religion and Health.*

I didn't have any expectations; I really just wanted it out of my life.

A couple of months later I had all but forgotten about having submitted the paper, but I got an email from the journal saying that they had made a few edits to the paper (including some formatting edits as well, no doubt) and had decided to publish it in their following fall edition.

That situation had a profound impact on me, partially because it was the first time I had been published but more so because I realized that I didn't have to be perfect in order to succeed. I was so obsessed with getting the paper and the formatting perfect that—for several months—I stayed stuck on the step of submitting it. This is when I coined a phrase for myself that has served me well ever since.

"Pro, not perfect."

Pro, meaning that I wanted to create products that were high quality and professional but not hold out until they are perfect, since perfection is an illusion.

I realized that I was getting stuck due to perfection-ism in many different areas of my life, not just this paper. Perfectionism was not what I thought it was. I thought it was being concerned about producing something that has value. If that were the only thing going on, then perfec-tionism would be no problem. I still want to do that—to create products with value. But there was another layer of perfectionism that I didn't understand, a racket that had a lot of payoffs toward staying safe, stuck, and unproductive.

As I look back now, I realize that I didn't want to sub-mit that paper to the journal for publication because I was terrified that it wouldn't get published. I was afraid that they would realize that I was what I thought I might be—stupid, a fraud, or someone who had slipped through the cracks and gotten into grad school but was now exposed for who I really was—an idiot. I was fearful about what it might *mean* if they "rejected" me. So, I would avoid working on it to continue to play small and live safely, not knowing whether the paper was publishable.

So, in order to avoid this racket I began to look at all my projects through the lens of "pro, not perfect." Since I want to do quality work but not stay stuck in fear of what people will think or say if it hasn't met my own standards of perfection, I get it to where I think it's at eighty percent of what it could be in its perfect form and then get feed-back, or just simply release it.

If failure is how we reach success, which I believe it is, then getting as many projects out there as possible for the scrutiny of others is a crucial step on the path toward where I want to be.

This same thing happens with singers all the time. They want to continue to work on their voice and not have anyone hear them until they reach a certain level of perfection, but this is a stuck place of safety and fear.

The same is true for a writer or someone who wants to launch a small business. At some point, and that point is well before you think it is, it has to go live in order for people to feel the impact of the service you are providing.

I was reminded of this principle when my business partners and I went to a movie release party for a Sci-fi Action/Adventure film that came out in 2010 called *Skyline*. Now this wasn't a critically acclaimed film, but the amazing thing about it was that they made it in a year (three years is the average, from script to screen) and for about a million dollars. Sure, that's a lot of money, but the effects looked as if they had a fifty- to a hundred-million-dollar budget, and the movie made nearly ninety million dollars.

Here's the thing that really struck my business partners and me. The filmmakers were all at the event and talked about the making of the film and said that since it wasn't a studio film but an independent film, they were very agile and able to approve graphics and processes very quickly, without all the red tape of a more corporate company. There were only a few people making all the decisions rather than twenty plus. In Director Strause's words from the stage that night, "There were only a few a**holes in the room making decisions rather than twenty a**holes." So when the monster graphics were reviewed along the way, and they didn't look *exactly* the way they wanted them to, they simply said, "Ah, that's good enough. Still looks great." Then they would move forward because they wanted to finish within the year because of the budget and also in order to release it as soon as possible. They weren't going to let perfectionism get in the way of getting this movie done and out into the public. They still made sure that it looked great but didn't get caught up in the minutia.

When my business partners and I adopted this principle, we moved so much faster and produced so much more. I would say that it's one of the main big ideas that caused SSM to be so successful. In fact, that event was enough of a milestone for us that we started using the word skyline as a verb; we said, "Skyline it," to mean, "It's good enough. Let's move forward and not allow this to bottleneck our process." In fact, we even named one of our umbrella companies "Skyline" as a constant reminder.

New Dreamers put themselves out there sooner, whether they fail or not. Often times we think we're not ready and that failure is assured if we release a product, but it often turns out that our work is much better than our inner critics let on. The only way we'll ever know is to skyline it. It can still be pro—professional and high quality—but doesn't have to be perfect, since perfection doesn't exist anyway.

15

It's Just a Game

*"When baseball is no longer fun,
it's no longer a game."*
~JOE DIMAGGIO

When we stay in the game, we succeed. It's that simple.

We tend to get out of the game and off our paths, either when we encounter what we consider to be a problem or obstacle or when we don't understand that we're playing a game. All of it is made up, and it's all just a game.

Saying that it's just a game doesn't mean that life and the pursuits of our goals and dreams are without meaning or that they make no difference; it means that there are a set of rules that manage our behavior just like in a board game or a game of baseball. And, of course, we can create or choose the game that we want to play at any point in time based on which set of rules appeals to us the most. This framework of rules is what makes the game fun and guides us on how to interact with others and accomplish goals.

Take baseball for instance. Growing up, I loved the game of baseball. I played little league, collected baseball cards, and went to Angels and Dodgers games with my dad. I understood all the rules of the game, which helped me stay engaged while watching and also follow what was going on as the game unfolded. In order to play baseball, you need to play within the framework of a set of rules and figure out how to be successful within those set parameters. So, in baseball, only the pitcher can throw the ball across the plate to the batter, and when the batter hits the ball it needs to stay within the ninety degree angle boundaries in order for it to be considered a hit, and then he has to run counter clockwise around the bases in order to get on base and eventually score.

New Dreamers refer to pursuits and activities as games, knowing that they have a way of awakening creativity and play. Games release us from the hold of how important and intimidating the projects are and put us back into control—without all the unnecessary and often paralyzing anxiety and fear that results from assigning too much significance to an endeavor.

The authors of *The Three Laws of Performance* write, "Play the game passionately, intensely, and fearlessly. But don't make it significant. It's just a game." Most of our pursuits are not matters of life and death. Now, New Dreamers certainly benefit from adding that kind of intensity and drive to the game, as long as the play aspect remains along the way. That's a great way to engage in the game—with intensity *and* play. But actually feeling as though the game is a matter of life and death creates panic and fear, and thus keeps us out of the game altogether, safely watching from the sidelines, hoping not to be called in to play.

Author and coach Steve Chandler uses an interesting exercise when working with Fortune 500 companies in which he splits the group in half and gives one group a serious "problem" to solve. Then, with the other group, he presents the task as a game instead of a problem and has them come up with the funniest or most absurd solutions. In this relaxed and creatively playful state, the second group nearly always comes up with superior actionable solutions in comparison to the ones hard at work trying to tackle the "problem." The playful group was accessing the right side of the brain, where all the good ideas emerge.

Referring to an activity as a game changes the way it occurs to us, and the way things occur to us radically affects our performance levels. This different way of thinking about a project tends to open up possibilities that previously didn't appear to exist. Within this gaming infrastructure a greater amount of opportunities begin to present themselves more clearly.

In their book, *The Art of Possibility*, Benjamin and Rosamund Zander write, "It is the nature of games to provide alternative frameworks for engagement and expression and growth, whisking us away from the grimmer context in which we hold the everyday."

When life and our chosen pursuits aren't fun anymore, this is an indicator that we're no longer playing a game. Instead of playing a game we often slip into fighting for survival, believing that money is oxygen and winning is the only way to stay alive. Comedian Groucho Marx says, "If you're not having fun, you're doing something wrong."

In what area of your life could you implement a greater dose of play by making it a game? One game could be called "Increasing my vocal range by two notes." This game can be played with any set of rules and parameters that you think would make it fun. Maybe you decide that winning the game means that you reach this goal within a month. Then you check to see what your vocal range is right now by using piano keys or maybe a guitar, and you write down where your vocal range is currently. Maybe you then decide that success will be most likely if you do your vocal exercises for a minimum of three days per week. But maybe you give yourself the freedom to choose any type of vocal exercises that you feel like doing on each given day, to keep things creative. Now you've got a game and a way to measure your results as you go along.

You may be thinking, "Well, if I make it a game, then I could lose, and I won't feel very good about myself if that happens." Part of the fun of a game is that you can lose. Being able to lose isn't a bad thing; it actually raises the stakes in a fun way that increases the challenge. Imagine playing a video game in which you couldn't lose; no matter what you did you would win. That would be fun for about three minutes, maybe. The very fact that you could lose makes the game worthy of effort, and it makes it far more exhilarating when you do win. It gives you an extra push of motivation each day as you play the game, knowing that you would really like to win and that that will come with a certain cost, commitment, and amount of discipline.

Maybe you want to play a longer-term game called "Top 10 on the Billboard charts." What might you have to shift in your life to make this a reality? What rules and guidelines will help ensure that these shifts take place? In this game, how will you measure progress along the way?

Whatever your pursuit, in whatever industry, making it a game helps New Dreamers not take things so seriously along the way. We can seriously, passionately, and intensely work towards it, but we don't need to give it significance; it is just a game, after all—not oxygen.

16
Get a Coach

"Everyone needs a coach.
It doesn't matter whether you're a basketball player,
a tennis player, a gymnast or a bridge player."
~BILL GATES

One great way to go further, faster in life is to hire a coach. We know this is true when it comes to sports, dance, singing, fitness, etc., but we don't necessarily think about it when it come to our lives. I remember I used to think, "Why would I need a 'life' coach? I know how to live life." I misunderstood what a coach was, and, incidentally, the results I was getting were attesting to the fact that I was an amateur at best when it came to living life and accomplishing my goals and dreams.

A good coach can help unearth and redesign thoughts and belief systems we have that get us the same "unwanted" results over and over again—rackets that we run on ourselves of which we're generally unaware. With an updated

GPS system, as we talked about earlier, we have a more direct route to getting new results in our lives.

I've seen the power of coaching over and over again in my own life and also in the lives of my clients. When I first began being coached, a new world that I never even knew existed opened up to me.

It was almost as if I were in London at King's Crossing Station around 9:30 AM on September 1st, and I walked into and through the wall ending up on platform 9 3/4 and eventually on the Hogwarts Express—for you Harry Potter fans. There was a preexisting world of possibility that had always been there to which I hadn't previously had access.

When I shifted my way of being, the world itself seemed to have changed. Within a year I was making four times as much money, I was light years closer to my deepest, truest dreams, and I went from a relatively stagnant dating relationship to an exciting marriage with the same woman—who is now my beautiful wife.

I realize that sounds like a too-good-to-be-true statement, partially because it's said without revealing the details of the painful process, and it also leaves out how much I am still in the process of my own growth. I was certainly ripe for some good coaching and was sitting on a winning lottery ticket in many ways, given all the opportunity I had had previously—much of which I was denying and/or squandering. I was so caught up believing my limiting voices about what a loser I was and how failure was all that the world had for me, that I was playing an embarrassingly small game, thinking that's all I was capable of doing.

As I began to live into my own deeper purpose, though, I found that I not only wanted to pursue a career as an actor and filmmaker but that I also wanted to help transform others' lives the way mine had been transformed. I had been in the business of transforming clients' singing voices, and now I wanted to do that on a larger scale—a more full-life scale. So I devoured every book about coaching I could get my hands on for a couple of years while continuing with my coaching, and then I started taking on clients of my own.

I was shocked and delighted to see my own clients' lives shift radically as well. One client, who is a marine biologist whom I'll call Jennifer, began dating after keeping men at bay for nearly fifteen years. She lost 20 pounds and has added speaker and success coach to her already successful career as a marine biologist; she recently signed her first two paid clients.

I believe in the power of coaching. Miracles happen when two minds come together to work on one life. And it's particularly effective if you get a coach when there are specific goals you want to accomplish in your life—ones that are measurable and that you are determined to go after together.

Do you want to become a better singer, painter, dancer, businessperson, or something else? Would you be willing to look into getting a coach or being coached through a class or a program? I've seen tremendous benefit from being coached one-on-one and also through classes and programs.

The pushback is often, "Well, yeah, I'm sure it would help, but I can't afford a coach." While I understand the reality of living with limited resources—I spent most of my life in that place—I also have, over and over and over again, seen, in my life and the lives of my clients, the power of cranking up one's desire and level of commitment and acquiring whatever is needed to attain our goals. It's okay if you can't afford it *today*. No problem. No shame. Are you willing to find out exactly how much it would take to get the program or the coach, write the figure down, and make a commitment to save up for it by a specific date and time?

I've found that good coaching always pays itself off by a large margin. And if I tell myself that I can't afford something, it usually means that I don't really, really want it or am unwilling to put in the work it takes to acquire it. And sometimes it just becomes a good excuse (a racket) for me to remain stuck in and use to fortify a case as to why it's impossible to succeed in a particular area—another way to limit my options and stay in the safety of inaction.

If we're serious about gaining a certain level of mastery in an area, the truth is that we can't afford not to get good coaching. Author, lawyer, and former Harvard University president Derek Bok states, "If you think education is expensive, try ignorance." This may seem like an offensive statement, but the truth is that investing in yourself and in your future is a great investment. You are worth it. Don't allow yourself to believe the limiting voices that tell you otherwise.

Our limiting voices create the boundaries of how big we allow our worlds to be. Believe in yourself and your own bigness. Believe in the possibility of a bigger world that you can live into.

A coach can help you with this.

New Dreamers understand that we go further and faster when we have coaches and can more quickly and easily course-correct or expose a blind spot that's keeping us off the path of success. That's why I still have a coach today...a few, actually.

17

Feedback

"We all need people who will give us feedback.
That's how we improve."
~BILL GATES

When I consider getting feedback, I internally brace for
the worst. This is no doubt a symptom of my recovering
pessimism. I think that the person giving the feedback will
confirm all the limiting voices in my head about how much
of a failure I am and how bad of a job I'm doing. I might
even trick myself into thinking that there is such a thing as
negative feedback and positive feedback, as if there were a
distinction and as if one were more valuable than the other.

If we can consider feedback to be neutral, not allowing "negative" or "positive" feedback to rattle us or puff us
up, then we have the opportunity to see both as potential resources. We can put the so-called positive feedback
in our "Truth About You" list, and we can see if there is a
constructive gift for us in the so-called negative feedback.

We may ask ourselves, "In light of this apparent criticism, where might I be able to shift that would open up greater resources and opportunity for me?" or, "That was said in anger, so I'm going to check back in with that person later and see what kind of truth was in there and what I could quickly discard."

Danish philosopher Søren Kierkegaard wrote, "To see yourself is to die, to die to all illusions and all hypocrisy. It takes great courage to dare to look at yourself…You must want only the truth, neither vainly wish to be flattered nor self-tormentingly want to be made pure devil." It is courageous to look at yourself and see your true impact on others, and as Kierkegaard notes, desiring the truth is the key to using feedback as a resource. Allow the truth to cut through the flattery seeking of the ego as well as any demonizing self-abasement. Truth gets us to current reality, to what really *is*, and once we're there, we can see clearly enough to get somewhere else that may be a greater resource to us and/or a greater service to humankind.

The other benefit of listening to what people say about us is finding some of our undiscovered strengths within comments we hear others say about us over and over again. If you notice that several people say the same thing to you, like, for example, "You have such a clear way of explaining things," then that might be a particular strength of yours. Hence, there may be some benefit to paying attention to that and working to develop your writing or speaking, since you've already found ways to connect easily with others. We're not always clued into the things we do well because they come easily to us, and we assume that the same strengths must apply to everyone.

Feedback helps us to have clear ideas of our actual impacts on others. There is nearly always a disconnect between our intentions, that is, the intended impact on another person, and the actual impact on that person. As we close the gap between our intentions and impacts, we become much more effective at whatever it is that we're doing.

For example, if you want to be a great singer but don't get feedback from a professional, or even simply allow someone else to hear you, you'll never have a clear idea of where you are and what techniques you may need to improve your skill. While feedback usually comes from a live person in your world, you can also acquire feedback by watching an instruction video or reading a book that teaches you a proper technique you can use to fix any mistakes you're making.

This is true for relationships as well. I remember that when my wife and I first were married, I had it in my head that a good husband would greet his wife at the door and then sit and listen to her, asking her about her day. So, that's what I did. I didn't mind doing this, but I was often in the middle of a thought, working on a project, editing a video, or whatever else it may have been, and would have liked ten or twenty minutes to wrap up before switching gears. This went on for a couple of months.

I don't remember how the conversation came up—I wasn't clued in enough to actually bring it up myself—but she told me that when she comes home she prefers to have twenty or thirty minutes to herself to decompress before diving into how her day went.

You see, my intention was to be a good husband and cause my wife to feel loved and heard. I didn't realize that my impact was causing more of a low-grade frustration for both of us, because I didn't stop to get some feedback from her earlier. So now that my intention and impact are more in alignment in that particular area, I'm more effective as a husband who wants to impact my wife in a certain way.

Most of us tend to have an inflated view of how effective we're actually being. This can be detrimental to our progress because we walk around with a large discrepancy between intention and impact and thus miss out on a huge percentage of our potential effectiveness, or our latent success. Feedback allows us to gain clearer perceptions of current reality—of how things really are. This is incredibly powerful because it's very difficult to get where we want to go without having a clear idea of where we are right now.

The mall is a good example. Let's say I parked out in front of Macy's and entered the mall, and after having visited a few stores I end up at the food court. As I'm ready to leave I see the Apple Store and remember I stopped in there not long after I arrived at the mall and feel like I have my bearings and head left, thinking that that's the direction toward Macy's. I keep walking until I reach that end of the mall and see Bloomingdales. I went the wrong direction. My bearings were not calibrated correctly after all. I didn't take the time to get feedback on current reality before choosing my direction. One way I could have gotten feedback was to find a mall map and search for the "You are here" sticker. That sticker represents a clear picture of current reality. Once we know what the current reality is, we can easily create a map to get to wherever else we want to go.

Current reality in life consists of our actual impacts on the world and the people in it. This gives us clarity of focus that provides the tools we need to go from where we are to where we want to be.

Asking others for feedback about particular areas in which we want to be stronger is a helpful New Dreamer practice. I regularly send out feedback forms to my coaching clients after a session because I know that my intention and impact are not always in alignment.

Another way to receive feedback is simply to be on the lookout for it. The world and the people in it are constantly giving us feedback that we can choose to be aware of if we pay attention.

I remember that my wife wasn't particularly engaged in the conversations that I was forcing when she came home from work, but I was so intent that this was the right thing to do that I didn't pick up on the non-verbal feedback that I was getting from her.

One common challenge to discovering the true nature of our current realities is our resistance to it. Often times our first impulse is to want to fight tooth and nail to defend our previously held position. We've held onto it for so long sometimes that it begins to feel like a trusted friend. Giving up our desire to be right can go a long way toward getting clear about current reality.

New Dreamers accept current reality as quickly as possible. This doesn't mean that we surrender to the fact that this is all that is possible, but rather that we surrender to the truth so that we can have a clearer idea of how to go from where we currently are to where we want to be.

Where in your life would you like to be more effective, more successful, or more powerful? Are you willing to seek out some verbal feedback from the person(s) that could help you get a clearer idea of your actual impact? Are you willing to write down three names right now and shoot them a text, email, or phone call?

It's nice to hear from people who you know like you, and that could be a great resource. It's sometimes even more resourceful to seek out at least one or two people who you know don't like you very much. While some of their feedback may be biting or extreme, there also may be a truth that comes from them that may be a real benefit to you.

We all need feedback…If we want to improve, that is.

18

The Machine

*"There are plenty of difficult obstacles in your path.
Don't allow yourself to become one of them."*
~RALPH MARSTON

I often say that I started college later than most people,
but that's not really true. I actually started going to college
earlier than most, at seventeen years old, since my birthday
is in August and I graduated high school in June, before
my eighteenth birthday.

My first attempt to go to college was a fail, so to speak.
I signed up for three classes at Orange Coast College, a
community college in Orange County, California. Not fully
understanding the necessity of general education courses,
and only being interested in singing and music, I signed up
for a keyboard class, a guitar class, and an ear-training singing class (I had always wanted to have perfect pitch and to
be able to name any key without the help of an instru-
ment or tuning fork—I still don't and can't). That college

endeavor lasted about three weeks. Since I had been living on my own for several months by that time and needed to continue working full time to pay rent and bills, going to college and supporting myself proved to be too much for me to juggle.

I gave college another go—more successfully this time—five years later. The second time around, I put graduating into my Commitment Compartment and had made a decision that nothing would stop me from accomplishing this goal, not even the fact that I had less than one hundred dollars to my name.

My college had a great incentive program. If I were able to maintain a 3.7 GPA or above, all my tuition would be covered, half by the college and the other half through grants and scholarships. So I saw my studies as a way to not only excel in school but also as a way to keep me from having to get a job, which could be too much to handle along with school work, as it had been before.

I also found that I was far more productive in the library, with fewer distractions, than I was at a coffee shop or in the communal spaces on campus. I spent so much time in the library during the day that some of my friends nicknamed me "The Machine." While it wasn't the most flattering nickname in the world, there was something in it that resonated with me—something positive that I kept.

I realized that when I wanted something so badly that I was determined to have it no matter what—when it was deeply rooted in my Commitment Compartment—there was an almost robotic part of me that emerged. When this part of me kicked in, I would immediately shut down any limiting voices that were clamoring, and choose to add more love into whatever I needed to do in order to accomplish my goal. It's almost like I would create a map in my mind of what needed to be done and then follow it like a soldier in battle no matter what challenge came at me, from within or from outside.

This didn't mean that I would shut off my emotions toward other people, of course; in fact, no matter how deep into the library I would go to study at a cubicle, or how often I would change where I set up shop to study in the library, my friends would always find me, and the cubicle chair next to mine would become the seat of my counselees who needed some direction or solace. I didn't shut my emotions off toward others but toward myself to override limiting thoughts and desires for comfort.

The primary emotion I flexed was a choice to love what I was reading and learning and to add more love and interest into whatever task I was doing—a task leading me to the future that I had committed myself to attain.

This robotic sense of focus came in very handy my sophomore year when my girlfriend of two years ended our relationship. At the time I was devastated; I mean, *really* devastated. It hit me harder and caused me to experience more emotion than I had in any previous event up until—or really since—then. In fact, I wrote and recorded a five-song EP about it. It was a very Dashboard

Confessional-esque, Emo album called "Unsent Letters: The Princeton EP."

This may sound a little bit insane (and very well may have been), but I wept daily, throughout most of the day, for three straight weeks and then several days a week for the two to three months following. It was as if this breakup breached the walls of the dam that held back all my repressed emotions from childhood to that day, and the tears were not going to stop until every disappointment and hurt was properly (and completely!) grieved.

As you can imagine, this was not a very conducive environment for being a successful student, maintaining normalcy in my life, and keeping up my 3.7 GPA. So, while my emotions were completely out of control, I, in a rare sane moment, created a mental map of all the things that I was committed to do no matter how miserable and hopeless I felt—I needed to wake up at the same time everyday, eat regular meals, exercise, go to class, and do homework.

Now these are very basic actions, but you have to understand, I couldn't care less about anything in my life at that point. Nothing seemed to matter to me at all more than my grief, and giving up on life altogether felt like a great plan. My limiting voices were all shouting simultaneously at the top of their lungs. But some grounded part of me still knew that giving up was a stupid plan.

So, I robotically went through the motions of doing healthy things in spite of how little I, in the moment, cared about my future. I knew that this would eventually pass—even though it lasted an absurd amount of time—and I could either work later to attempt to put the pieces of my life back together, or I could wake back up into a life that was firing on all cylinders and heading toward my original vision for my life.

Well, after many weeks of holding back tears in class and heading straight to the school chapel to be alone and cry between classes, it eventually did pass. When I awoke from that intense grief period I was happy that I had continued with the basic, healthy disciplines that seemed to hold my life together. And through that I learned a New Dreamer principle that has stuck with me. There is a robotic side of you and me that can serve us in our pursuits of our visions and goals in life.

Back then it felt almost like allowing a survival method to kick in, and while life isn't like that for me now, there is still a battle that rages in my mind daily that has the potential of kicking me off the path toward fulfilling my dreams. When I recognize this battle against distraction and limiting voices, I can use that same mechanism of relentlessly choosing to stay on the path that will yield the results that I most want.

This battle isn't a battle of resistance; it's about recognizing the presence of limiting voices and making a declaration beforehand that you will choose to stay on the path even in the face of potential diversions.

We all have a robotic side of us that can be leveraged into accomplishing our goals, the side of us that says, "I will not go to bed tonight before doing my vocal routine, no matter what," or, "I'll finish writing two pages of my book today no matter what comes up, no matter how I feel, no matter how loud the limiting voice in my head screams, 'It won't matter; you'll never get it published.'"

It begins with a choice, not a "should" or a "try" or an "I'd really like to one of these days" but a definitive choice. After this choice, it's a matter of robotically working on the task whether we feel like it or not. Once we start it gets easier, and once we've done it for long enough the momentum fulcrum kicks in and then a habit forms, but the robot within helps us to get to that place. The robot is the helper that gets us from inaction to the first rewards of being on the path, and the next phase is momentum and habit, where we're doing far less and seeing far more results.

When we get crystal clear about what it is we want and decide to work for it, our energy and motivation toward that action increases. We have a choice to engage our inner robotic sides and give something laser focus.

The freakishly emotional semester I had was the one just before my junior year—when the faculty asked me to teach the class to the incoming freshman class about how to form and maintain good study habits.

That's a nice happy ending to the story, but I wonder what would have happened if I had let my emotions and temporary hopelessness take control for those two to three months rather than using my inner robotic drive to choose and follow a path that would yield a more resourceful outcome no matter how I felt.

That decision set me on a path that led to acceptance into my first choice graduate school. You see, the decisions we make today are not always just passing decisions; they very often form a path, and each path has a series of results—some paths lead to results we want and others... well, not so much.

We don't have to wait until there is a crisis in our lives in order to make use of the resources we have within ourselves and create the lives that we want. And the truth is that many of us are in more of a crisis than we are currently aware. Yes, we occasionally feel the weight of putting very little time into the things that we tell ourselves and others we really want, but it fades as we keep ourselves over-scheduled and too busy to notice.

This isn't a judgment, by any means; this is a confession and awareness of how I gave away about a decade or so of my life avoiding a genuine pursuit of my dreams because of my own desire for comfort. It's a confession of how I often abandon all New Dreamer principles and give my days away as I listen to, and believe, my own limiting voices that clamor to keep me safe and comfortable. All breakthroughs in our lives exist outside of our comfort zones, so when I stay inside of my comfort zone I can't have breakthroughs in my life that will lead to a future worth having.

So now I see a crisis as anytime I remain consistently off the path, since success can only be found by staying on the path. If I'm regularly off the path, I'm keeping success at bay indefinitely until I wake up and get back on. So I use the robotic side of me on a regular basis to throw me back onto the path for a few days or weeks until the habit is rebooted.

The path is the plan we've set out for ourselves in a particular endeavor. It's the logical path that follows cause and effect. It's sitting in front of the computer every day if you want to be a writer; it's attending regular classes if you want mastery over your craft. The path is not difficult to discover, it's getting derailed from the path that is generally our greatest challenge.

For example, if I realize that I've let my eating habits slip for several days or weeks in a row (which happens often) in small ways that are beginning to look like a pattern (usually that means I've eaten ice cream several days in row, and now I'm craving sugar everyday!), then I'll reboot myself back onto the path by saying, "Okay, I will have a strict no-junk-food diet for five days in a row." I'll say it aloud, tell my wife and my coach, write it down, and then choose to do it, robotically, no matter how I feel about it or what I think I want in the moment. I don't need to be in this machine-like mode for long. Then before long I'm back on the path and momentum continues to propel me forward.

When in your life have you experienced this robot-like focus? What was it that got you into it? In what area would your inner machine serve you in moving toward your purpose, stated goals, and vision? Whether you need to start something from scratch and forge a brand new path or you need a kick in the butt to get you back onto a path that you've strayed from, you can use your robotic side to get the gears turning. Where might you be off the path and haven't quite realized it yet?

Are you willing to choose right now to jump back on and robotically take the necessary steps without checking in on your emotions to see if you feel like it and without paying attention to any limiting voices?

PART 5

HEALTHY
LIVING

19

Faster, Slower

"Going faster doesn't really help
when you are going in the wrong direction."
~Michael Neill

When I was in graduate school I remember reading a book called *Faster* by James Gleick in which he mentions that the "DOOR CLOSE" buttons in elevators in Japan are the only ones with the paint worn off. I thought that was an interesting and humorous way to talk about their hurried culture. I finished reading for the day, deep in the basement of the Princeton University library, and got into the elevator. As I pressed the button to go up to the ground floor, I noticed that the "DOOR CLOSE" button in that elevator was not only devoid of paint, but the bottom half of it was also worn down about a quarter inch, while all the other buttons appeared nearly untouched. It resembled a stone that had been worn away by rushing water over the course of several years.

Life and technology seem to be moving faster and faster, and in order to "keep up," we tend to become busier and busier, packing our schedules to the gills and exhausting ourselves. In fact, I've started noticing that when I ask people how they're doing or how life is going, the most common answer tends to be, "Busy!"

I'm all for accomplishing a lot. In fact, the first coaching company name that my colleague and I came up with is ATP: Addicted To Progress. Watching projects move forward invigorates me, which is why I focus so much energy on helping my clients get unstuck so that they can get back on the path of progress toward their goals as soon as possible.

The madness, though, comes when we believe the lie that I believed for the better part of my life, and still sometimes fall prey to: that speeding up, putting more on my plate, and stressing myself out is the way toward progress. I thought that hard work and grinding out my days was the way to reach my goals.

Working hard has value and will produce a certain amount of results, no question. But the tyranny of more and more and more hard work has a ceiling, and that ceiling is pretty low. Life at that speed tends to lead to burnout, lack of peace, and a lot of spinning of our wheels.

The Pareto Principle (the 80/20 rule), of which you may already be familiar, offers some insight into this. It says that roughly eighty percent of the effects in our lives (wealth, good relationships, accomplishing of our dreams, etc.) come from twenty percent of the causes. So, in other words, only twenty percent of the actions we take during the day produce eighty percent of the results we're getting. Yet, we keep piling on more and more without stopping to examine which activities are part of the result-producing twenty percent. So most actions end up accumulating in the wheel-spinning eighty percent that is having little effect beyond cranking up our stress level and blood pressure. It makes a lot of sense that Socrates said in his now famous quotation, "The unexamined life is not worth living."

There is a whole other level of possibility when we choose to slow down in order to speed up—to carve out space in our lives for rest and play. When we do, we give our minds a chance to get off of the same thoughts we're rehearsing over and over again and have some fresh ideas—some newness that will lead to inspiration and wisdom. It only takes a handful of really good ideas per year to create a very prosperous life. But if we're always running one hundred miles an hour and allowing the same thoughts and fears to run our lives, then those fresh ideas will remain underneath the surface, buried in the subconscious.

So, what's the alternative? How can we get these fresh thoughts and ideas to come to the surface so that we can live more productive lives while doing less and slowing down?

One tool for slowing down to speed up is silence. Brilliant French physicist and writer Blaise Pascal says, "All of humanity's problems stem from man's inability to sit quietly in a room alone." And this doesn't mean that you need to become a monk and sit silently for hours at a time. Starting with even a few minutes of this type of meditation will begin to add a level of peace and insight into your life that will begin to radically increase your effectiveness. Author, coach, and multi-millionaire businessman Sam Beckford says, "Silence is the factory in which greatness is created."

I noticed a far greater sense of peace in my life when I implemented this into my schedule. I'm not always consistent and perfect with this, but I often spend at least ten to fifteen minutes in solitude in the morning. It's a good way to get centered and focused, and it helps me get perspective on the fearful thoughts that usually fill my mind when I first wake up in the morning.

It also becomes a place where ideas surface organically—ideas that tend to save me time and energy by giving me a clearer road map for my day. Being a big fan of progress and results, I want to eliminate high-effort low-return activities (which I'm guessing is the same for you). But it took me most of my life to realize that slowing down, getting present, and connecting to my highest set of priorities was a great way to get what I was after. The 16th century German author and reformer Martin Luther said, "I have so much to do that I shall spend the first three hours in prayer."

It's amazing what kinds of resourceful thoughts will come to the surface during this time. And it doesn't have

to be sitting in a room, though I definitely recommend trying that; the same thing can happen as you go for a walk
or take a drive in your car with no particular destination.
As we use the simple motor skills of walking or driving, we
occupy the left side of the brain—the logical, analytical,
judgmental side—and free up the right side of the brain—
the creative, intuitive side, where all great ideas are waiting
for us to slow down long enough for them to emerge and
give us the insights that will lead to fuller, freer lives.

This same New Dreamer principle applies when you
go on vacation, too, since that's another time when we typ-
ically allow our minds to take a break from all the thoughts
and anxieties of daily life. This allows us to see past all the
chaos that takes up the bandwidth of our minds and sup-
presses the creative brilliance that exists in all of us.

There is a way of being that shows up when our mind
isn't clouded with the seriousness and anxiety that comes
from grinding it out day after day. In this state of play—
relaxed and creative—brilliance has a chance to emerge,
and not just for the elite or the most intelligent or the most
successful people—it is available to everyone.

I remember a couple years ago sitting in a coffee shop
with one of my business partners, who has been one of
my closest friends since college. He's naturally really funny,
so we were laughing and joking and hanging out. At one
point he pulled out his computer to show me our new-
est piece of marketing content for SSM that was almost
done. It was an animated doodle video for which I had

done the voiceover track about a month prior. We were to give the overseas doodle video company our final notes and tweaks. We watched it, and it looked really great, except every time our company name was written in the video, it said "Superior *Signing* Method" instead of "Superior *Singing* Method." Still being in a silly state of play, I jokingly said, "We should build another program about how to do sign language and call it 'Superior *Signing* Method.'"

He laughed, thought for a second, and then quickly jumped online to check out all the analytics for how much traffic sign language searches were getting, what resources were currently available, and how much the competition was marketing for it. It looked like a wide-open market. Fast forward to now—the time of writing this book, that is—and we have a full sign language course, a baby sign language course, and a seven-thousand-word sign language dictionary. We decided to change the name to Signing Success, and we've been affectionately calling it our retirement.

Whenever we relax, laugh, or play, we are in a quiet state of mind. Whenever we simply see through our serious thinking, we tap into these insights, which are always available to us. This wisdom and insight are always present. We tend to cloud our minds with so many thoughts and worries and strategies and fears that we get derailed from this understanding that would serve us and help us more powerfully serve the world.

The inspiration that bubbles up to the surface from inside is such that by using it we make far more progress in a matter of hours than we would in several months of hard work and struggle. All of our thoughts, worries, and limiting voices about making more money and reaching our dreams and being in the right relationships are the very things that are hindering us from gaining access to these insights and ultimately to what we want in our lives.

Slowing down helps us to let go of those thoughts, of that restrictive way of thinking. When we do, our natural wellbeing and wisdom are allowed to shine through again, and it's in this space that miracles happen, because people who are happy and at peace are more successful. Allowing ourselves to slow down and enjoy our lives and do the things we really love to do creates the kind of environment that is a breeding ground for miracles, financial prosperity, better relationships, and the accomplishment of our dreams.

The worries are what blocks our connection to this flow of wisdom, and this worried, stressful state comes directly from our thoughts and limiting voices. New Dreamers recognize that we are living in the feelings of our thinking and not the feelings of our circumstances. That may sound confusing, so let me give you an example.

Let's say I wake up in the morning and look out the window to find that the sky is filled with dark clouds, and it's pouring down rain. All of a sudden I start *feeling* sad and maybe even a little depressed. In that moment, I would be tempted to believe that the rain (the circumstance) *caused* me to feel sad and depressed. It may seem to me that this circumstance had a direct link to my feelings. Then let's say that you walk to the window, see the same thing, but feel excited and relieved. You may also think that the rain is making you feel these things.

But the brain is not wired that way. Circumstances don't have a direct link to our feelings, even though that's often how it appears. Only our thoughts have that direct link to our emotions.

So let's take a deeper look at what's going on here, at what stressful, limiting voices may have been clamoring inside my head. When I went to the window and saw the rain I was maybe thinking, "This is going to make traffic worse," or, "It's so gloomy; I'd rather not leave the house at all today, but I really don't feel like I could miss this meeting," or, "I knew I should've replaced my broken umbrella," or something like that.

You, on the other hand, see the rain and think, "How refreshing," or, "How soothing and relaxing," or, "This is going to be great for my garden and really help the drought."

You see, while both you and I think the rain is making us feel a certain way, it's actually our thoughts about the rain, the *meaning* we add to the rain (the circumstance), that causes the feelings. That is why the rain seems to cause different feelings in different people, because it's occurring to each person differently depending on their thoughts surrounding it and the meaning they are automatically adding to it.

We end up spending so much time attempting to alter the circumstances in our lives without understanding that the unwanted feelings we're getting are simply from our own thoughts. And since our thoughts are just made up stories, we have infinitely more options of what to think about.

It's not necessarily about replacing the thought with another more positive one, but understanding that you always have the choice of which thoughts to focus on and repeat. This understanding alone allows you to let stressful thoughts go, since they're all made up anyway.

When we slow down to the actual speed of life and we breathe deeply into the present moment, we tend to have a much easier time letting go of those limiting voices (e.g. I need more money or I don't deserve any better than this), getting centered again, and back into this flow of wisdom.

Now all of that flow of wisdom stuff may sound strange to you, but it's in line with most faith traditions. If this hasn't been your experience, I'd challenge you to test it out. You can refer to the flow of wisdom as Spirit or Holy Spirit or God or the Universe or Higher Power, but there is some type of organized intelligence in each of us to which we have access when we slow down, release all the repeating fearful thoughts and allow the fresh thinking and insights to come to the surface.

The nice thing about these insights that bubble up from inside us is that they are nearly always immediately actionable. We don't have to drum up the motivation to get into the action they inspire. They are often ready to go.

Once we are clear about what the next move is, we move, and when we do move, we move in the right direction. New Dreamers don't need to move quickly but simply take the next small step—whatever is needed in the present moment to move an insight closer to fruition.

20

Renewal

"Sleep is the best meditation."
~Dalai Lama XIV

Another great way to slow down is to give your body enough sleep.

When I was in graduate school I took a course called "Sleep, Surrender, Sabbath." It seemed like a pretty cushy, interesting psychology course, but it ended up having a profound impact on my life and some of my habits that have remained to this day.

In the class, all of the students were encouraged to choose and commit to an experiment for the duration of the semester, alongside the required reading and paper writing for the course. The first book I read was called *The Promise of Sleep* by William C. Dement, an American pioneer in sleep research, in which he wrote about the sleep debt that everyone carries around with them. He said that for every minute of sleep less than eight hours and fifteen minutes per night, a sleep debt accumulates, and that the average human being carried around a minimum of fifty hours of sleep debt, which affects mood, productivity, clarity of thought, creativity, health, and happiness. Having read this, I decided to do what I could over the course of the eight to ten weeks left in the semester to make up as much as possible of the sleep debt I was carrying and chronicle the effects over time.

I blacked out the windows in my cozy, little dormitory and allowed myself to sleep as long as I could every night. By the end of the semester, the results were drastic. Everything felt different. Colors seemed brighter, my cognition was far clearer, my mood was much better, I became irritated far less easily, and I was just overall happier and more joyful. I felt great.

The other thing I discovered about myself was that the reason I hadn't chosen to sleep a greater amount of hours per night for the previous five or so years was my own fear that I wouldn't be able to survive and get ahead in life if I took regular time off and didn't work an insane amount of hours everyday. I was constantly rehearsing a pessimistic outlook of scarcity that compelled me to work to the point of exhaustion on a regular basis.

This was particularly true in college and then in graduate school, where I felt as though I didn't have what it took to excel, so I had to work many more hours than everyone else. This wasn't necessarily true, but my belief that it was dictated the actions I took, which turned me into a border-line workaholic.

I never forgot about that sleep experiment, and while I certainly don't get a full eight hours and fifteen minutes of sleep every night I have significantly increased the amount of sleep I schedule for myself. I sleep much more than I did back then, and I still have all my needs taken care of and then some. Turns out I didn't need to fight and struggle and work insane hours in order to survive after all. That was just a limiting voice born of a scarcity mindset that created a reality for me that was self-imposingly tyrannical.

Where in your life could you create some space for renewal? If you find yourself tired regularly, will you consider adding some downtime—some sanity—into your schedule? Will you consider allowing yourself more sleep at night, if you're lacking sleep now? Are you willing to believe that you'll still have what you need (and probably much more) if you take some time off? What small change are you willing to make today?

21

I'm Overwhelmed

"The key is not to prioritize what's on your schedule,
but to schedule your priorities."
~Stephen Covey

Do you ever feel overwhelmed?

Silly question, right?

I certainly do.

What I often fail to remember when I'm in the throes of feeling overwhelmed is that it is exactly that—a feeling.

When we're overwhelmed we feel as though life's challenges and responsibilities are pressing in on us; but in actuality it's our thoughts—our limiting voices—and, more specifically, believing that our thoughts represent concrete reality that produces the feeling of being overwhelmed.

For example, when I feel overwhelmed I'm usually thinking something like, "I have more on my plate than I can possibly accomplish today," or, "I don't know how I'm going to accomplish this task I've set out to do, and, in fact,

I don't even think I'm qualified or have the wherewithal to figure it out." It becomes less about the circumstance itself and more about my thoughts about the circumstance and the stories I make up surrounding it, and, more particularly, my thoughts about myself and my inability to handle it.

The feeling of being overwhelmed doesn't show up until the brain interprets and creates a story about a situation. So being overwhelmed (as well as feeling sadness, frustration, depression, and anxiety) can only happen when we see a situation, create an interpretation, and then believe that interpretation to be true.

We can only be overwhelmed by our thoughts about something, never by the thing itself. The *meaning* we add to the circumstance is what creates the feeling. Those thoughts might be, "This is bad for me," or, "I wouldn't be able to handle it if this thing happened."

All of this thinking tends to lead us to study the feelings associated with our thoughts, which is what generally leads to procrastination. We tend to mull around in our feelings rather than simply getting into action toward the thing by which we feel overwhelmed. We think, "I've got so much to do that I don't even know what to do next, so I'll do nothing," or, "I deserve a break, and it can't all get done anyway, so just forget the whole thing, at least for now."

But the problem with procrastination is that it breeds more procrastination and increases our fear about whatever it is that we are putting off—since it's action that alleviates fear. Procrastination itself produces a feeling of exhaustion and a low mood that decreases your confidence in your ability to accomplish things that matter. So, when we wake up the next day, after having procrastinated the day before, we feel sluggish and incomplete and even further overwhelmed by our to-do lists because our energy is low, which causes us to conclude that we're too tired to really accomplish much. It becomes a vicious cycle.

We tend to forget that we are the ones creating our to-do lists, which is evidenced by the fact that we often act like we're victims of our own schedules. We can choose what we deem important. We don't *have* to keep the jobs we have; we don't *have* to go to that family gathering; we don't *have* to answer every ding and alert from all our various devices. We *choose* to. When we say we're overwhelmed, the implication is that these choices are out of our hands. The statement itself is a statement of powerlessness. Even the prefix "over" in *over*whelmed seems to indicate that we're under something, being pressed in on and nearly crushed.

New Dreamers understand that we have the choice to create our days and boldly protect our time or simply respond and react to life's circumstances as they arise. We have so many opportunities throughout our days to absorb others' expectations and requests, whether it's phone calls, texts, emails, or anything else. There are infinite opportunities to get off track and off task with Facebook, Instagram, Twitter, Candy Crush, and whatever new social networking and gaming options exist by the time you read this. All of these things may be laughable by then like MySpace is now, but there will always be something tugging away at our time, in competition for our attention.

All of these things can be like the sharks in Hemingway's novel *The Old Man and the Sea*, constantly eating small chunks of Santiago's eighteen-foot marlin he caught and strapped to the side of his little skiff boat. By the time he reached the shore, the marlin's flesh was completely picked to the bone. Sometimes that's how I feel about my so-called priority for the day (my big catch)—my book writing or script memorization or whatever it is. When I allow all the distractions and requests to chip away at my time, instead of boldly prioritizing the tasks associated with my vision for the day, then I end up with a pile of bones and none of the meat of progress toward my stated vision. If I habitually do this day after day, I'll never accomplish the major goals and dreams in my life.

This takes us back to the conversation of *being* versus *doing*. When our being—our vision—is crystal clear, then it becomes much more apparent which activities and requests are not going to be resourceful in order for us to accomplish our primary objectives. The stronger our "yes" is to the clear vision that we're pursuing, the easier it is to say "no"—the easier it is to *recognize* when something is a "no."

Author and entrepreneur Derek Sivers takes this idea one step further and says that opportunities in his life fall into two categories: "Hell Yeah!" or a clear "no." I love this because it takes some of the guessing out of whether an opportunity is really good for me. When I ask myself which of these two categories a situation or opportunity falls under, I'm able to more powerfully create my day (and therefore my life) by cutting out all the things that are *good* in order to focus on the one or two projects that are *great*—the ones that I really, really want in my life. Because, as French writer and philosopher Voltaire says, "Good is the enemy of great."

There is a seemingly infinite amount of *good* opportunities that come up every day that are potentially fun or helpful or interesting but are a sidetrack from the primary thing that we're committed to that will lead to the future that we want—the *great* opportunities. This is why *good* is the enemy of *great*. A distraction that we're not interested in is not the enemy; we can quickly brush that to the side and continue forward with our stated commitments. But a *good* opportunity that's shiny and sexy is the enemy because of its attractiveness and allure. It's much easier to justify getting off track for something like that. But if we're not cognizant of the fact that the *good* is always waiting around the corner, offering one more reason to avoid the *great* work we're up to, then we can spend an entire lifetime not having completed the most important projects that give us a future worth having.

The more crystal clear we are about what is a "no" and what is a "yes," and the more often we choose only the

"Hell Yeah" options, the less overwhelmed we feel. Because feeling overwhelmed is not always simply connected to having too much on our plates or having too many distractions; it is often the result of having too many activities that are misaligned with what we love, what gives us life, and what infuses us with passion and energy.

While feeling overwhelmed ultimately stems from a thought believed, there are bold steps we can take in order to make these thoughts and stories less of a temptation to indulge in. It's nearly impossible to feel overwhelmed when we are in action doing the things we love that are furthering the goals of our stated visions. It's when we get out of action and back into our thoughts and worries that the feeling of being overwhelmed creeps back in and puts us into a stuck place.

When I'm feeling overwhelmed—which happens more often than I'd like to admit—and in a rare moment I choose to interrupt the feeling and simply get started on my project, I find that it's almost impossible to feel overwhelmed once I'm five or ten minutes deep into my work. This is a New Dreamer principle we talked about in the first chapter of this book…and it's one of the best ways to fight the feeling of being overwhelmed: The mind makes all future tasks seem bigger and scarier than they actually are, so just a couple minutes of action toward the thing you're avoiding is the way out of feeling overwhelmed by it.

What are your priorities? What gives you life? What are the activities that make you feel strong? As we intentionally schedule these things into our lives and boldly fight off distractions and the "good," we begin to create a future worth having, one that is filled with the things we want most in life.

Everyone has a to-do list, whether literally or figuratively. Are you willing to write down a "to-don't" list, a list of all the possible things that you could do and have a good quality to them but are ultimately a distraction from the things that would truly bring about the life that you desire? You can place this list next to your to-do list to remind you that you are doing great work and can't downgrade to take care of the merely *good* things right now. You may get to them later, but for now you're going to stick with the most important things and courageously say "no" to every other time- and energy-sucker. If our priorities are not scheduled, a thousand other options will take their place…every time.

22

I'm Worried

*"A day of worry is more exhausting
than a week of work."*
~John Lubbock

One habit that puts us in a stuck place and makes it difficult for us to move forward and be successful is worry. For much of my life I considered worry to be an important activity. I was never really aware that that was how it was occurring to me, and I never would have described it that way, but in retrospect that seems to have been one of my motivating factors. I know that sounds crazy, but it seemed foolish and irresponsible *not* to worry about things. I thought, "I worry because I care."

I associated worry with some form of strategizing, even when it produced nothing more than paralysis and fear. I was allowing my mind to project worst case scenarios, and I wasn't interrupting the thoughts but instead hanging onto them, as though that would somehow be a way to solve whichever issue it was that I was worrying about. This is insane thinking, but I've discovered that while many wouldn't necessarily articulate it this way, there is a sense for many that worry is a habit of those who are responsible. It's a mindset and a habit that I'm still frequently tempted to fall back into.

New Dreamers see that when we worry, we head down the path of reduced creativity, reduced imagination, reduced resourcefulness, and reduced possibility. And the ironic thing is that this lower state of being which produces a low mood, and lack of creativity cultivates the results we were so worried we might encounter.

If I'm worried about my finances and this worry puts me into a mild depression in which I can't see possibility as clearly and I stay inactive instead of serving others and being creative, then my financial situation will very likely decline. I helped to create this outcome with my worry.

To take it a step further, when what we're worrying about does come to pass, we're tempted to think, "Well, I was right to worry about it; it happened just as I thought it would." We can't see that we contributed to the undesired outcome through our own excessive worrying.

Another aspect of worry is that most people think they worry because of outside circumstances; for example, they worry because they anticipate bad things are on the horizon. Maybe you get a stomachache, and after some time it doesn't go away. You think, "Yes, I've got insurance, but it's still going to cost more than I have to spare right now."

You notice your mood start to sink, and then you think, "I don't make nearly enough money at my job. I feel like I'm never going to break out of living from paycheck to paycheck. What's wrong with me? Why does this stuff always happen to me?"

Oh, and you're not done. This train of thought causes you to be distracted from your work, and you go onto WebMD and see that your symptoms resemble that of pancreatic cancer, and you think, "This is not only going to cost me a ton of money, since my deductible is so high, it's going to cost me tons of time and maybe even my life." This is extreme, but the mind has no problem making huge leaps that don't serve us.

In that moment, we think that the stomachache has caused this worry and this low mood—that it has tapped into our emotions and is bringing us down. But what we often don't see is that the circumstance has no direct connection to our emotions; only our thoughts about something can have an impact on our feelings, a New Dreamer principle we saw in the previous chapter.

We worry not because of outside circumstances; we worry because we've gotten into the habit of worrying. It may be because worrying feels like the responsible thing to do or it may simply be because the victim mindset is the default position of the brain unless we proactively choose another one.

Worry is connected to a victim mindset, since it usually carries along with it some form of complaint about how powerless we are, or at least how powerless our lives seem to be. A complaint is usually a red flag that there is a racket present, and the victim mindset is married to the racket.

In the above example, she feels victimized by her financial situation, and her complaint is that she doesn't make enough money and that there is probably something wrong with her. Rackets, worries, and complaints have a symbiotic relationship; they work together to fortify the victim position so that we can continue to live in the payoffs of the rackets we're running. And if we can see this, we can begin to interrupt them and get different results in our lives.

Worry is also often connected to *forecasting*. Forecasting is assigning meaning to something that hasn't even happened yet. In the above example our fictitious woman quickly assigned the stomach ache the meaning that she didn't have the capacity to get a new job or earn a comfortable living and that there was something inherently wrong with her (not to mention that death may be imminent!). This is most likely not true, but whether it is or not, it's not a resourceful assignment of meaning; therefore, it would benefit her to choose another meaning to assign to the stomachache.

We make up meanings all the time. New Dreamers keep in mind that every situation has multiple meanings, and we have a choice of which meaning to assign to it. Unfortunately, we often choose the most negative meaning because it resonates with our limiting voices and internal conversations. But we can choose whichever meaning we want, so why not choose the one that most aligns with our dreams?

Let's look at another example of worry connected with forecasting. We might get an email from a potential client that says, "I'm not able to make the meeting tomorrow. Can we reschedule for next week?" and immediately feel discouraged and think, "She canceled the meeting, so she must not like me and not really want to work with me. Now I'm worried not only about the relationship but also about this project and how, or if, it's going to happen." This is certainly one possible meaning to assign to the email. I would argue that it's not a particularly resourceful one. If we can slow down and notice the meaning that we're assigning to circumstances throughout the day, we can put a dent in our worries and also get a glimpse into our limiting voices and rackets.

Most people make a direct correlation between worry and stress, as if they were synonymous. But worry *isn't* a form of stress. Worry is a form of anxiety. Stress is a different animal. Stress actually carries along with it some benefits. When we turn up the heat of stress, it tends to give us a sense of urgency that leads to action. This type of stress is called *eustress*. Without any eustress in our lives around a particular project, we generally lack the motivation to get started.

This is one of the reasons it's so important to make clear-cut goals and make ourselves accountable by sharing these goals with others and turning the project into a game with measurable milestones. This is a way to create some good stress in our lives, a self-imposed sense of imminence. New Dreamers make sure to always have some level of eustress surrounding a project that is going to lead to the fulfillment of their dream.

Stress is an upgrade from worry; anything that is going to get us into action and out of our heads is going to catalyze some type of change.

New Dreamers shift away from worry and upgrade it to something more actionable. One smaller upgrade would be to choose concern, which gets us out of the mindset of having no possibilities and causes us to ask more resourceful questions, like, "What can I do about this right now?" or, "What's good about this?" or, "In light of this circumstance, what would I like to create? Would I like to create a better relationship, a better product, or a better outlook?" or, "Am I speaking from a place of downward spiral thinking or from a place of possibility?"

Are you willing to take a minute or two right now and check in with yourself and see what worries might be brewing in the back (or even the forefront) of your mind? Which of these could you capture and take care of now? Are you willing to think about it in silence for ninety seconds and actually write down the things that are concerning you? Maybe there is the tiniest, little step you could take that would cause that project to occur to you differently and curb your anxiety about it. Maybe there is a request that you could make that would help move your vision forward, but you're worried that it's not going to go well. Are you willing to take one small step toward resolution of each of the worries on your list by the end of the day? Imagine how much extra bandwidth would open up in your mind once these worries began to drift away.

23

Exercise

"Physical fitness is not only one of the
most important keys to a healthy body,
it is the basis of dynamic and
creative intellectual activity."
~JOHN F. KENNEDY

New Dreamers recognize that exercise makes everything
in life better…but you've heard that enough times already.
You don't need me to repeat it.

24

How Can I Contribute?

"When you cease to make a contribution,
you begin to die."
~Eleanor Roosevelt

One of the greatest enemies of gratitude—and therefore of optimism as well—is greed. Now, I hesitate to even use the word "greed" instead of a word like "entitlement," which also applies, because greed is nearly impossible to recognize within ourselves. We don't usually have a problem recognizing it in others, but for us it's a different story. Part of the reason behind this is that when we think of the word "greed" we picture some fat-cat businessman who exploits the poor to increase his already massive wealth, like Mr. Potter in the movie *It's A Wonderful Life*.

Greed is subtler than that, though. At its core, it's simply a lack of appreciation for what we have—the mindset of "never enough." It's that red-faced spoiled kid in each of us that wants a new toy and wants it now. It's the scarcity mindset that drives us to accumulate and hoard—the way of thinking that there aren't enough resources to go around so we need to acquire everything we can.

Some are living in regions of the world where their lives are in danger daily and scarcity is the reality, but I'm speaking of the limitations of a scarcity mindset in a setting where resources are more abundant. The scarcity mindset is survival thinking, based on the belief that life is dangerous and daily survival is a struggle, and, therefore, looking out for "number one" is vital.

This type of thinking makes it far more difficult to enjoy all the rich benefits of gratitude and optimism, and, of course, the fulfillment and success of our dreams, goals, and missions. These ways of thinking feed the greedy, little miser that lives in each one of us.

One simple New Dreamer practice we can use to begin to shift our minds and create new, more resourceful habits is to change one of the questions we ask ourselves. Instead of asking, "What am I getting out of this?" we can ask ourselves, "How can I contribute?" This opens up a new way of relating to the people and circumstances around us. And, surprisingly, it's generally the way we end up getting the things we want and having the most fulfilling lives. Generosity has a way of changing us from the inside and making us more trustworthy, whole, and happy.

Success in any endeavor is much more likely to present itself when we shift our thinking to believe that there are always more opportunities available, and living a life of generosity—asking ourselves how we can be contributors—is the catalyst for this shift. When we choose to believe in an abundant world and act joyfully and generously, we tend to care much less about being in control and instead choose to take risks more often—both of which lead to greater resources in regards to relationships, finances, and accomplishing our chosen visions and dreams.

Until we shift our mindsets and choose to believe that we live in a generative and generous world, full of possibility, this scarcity mindset will always be in the backdrop of our lives, and no matter how much money we make, how much approval we get, or how much we accomplish, there will always be a dark cloud of fear hanging over us—a feeling that at any moment we may lose it all and not be able to handle it. This scarcity mindset is a byproduct of listening to, and choosing to entertain, the limiting voices in our heads.

Recognizing that I, like everyone else, have a resident greedy, little miser inside me—the epitome of a scarcity mindset—I decided to create a systematic action that would starve him out and open up a new way of thinking for me. I began to set aside a percentage of my income to give to communities and causes that I believe in and then another separate percentage to give away in any way that would be generous. This is a practice that my wife and I still use today; we call it our "Gen Fund" (Generosity Fund).

Now, don't get me wrong; this was a painful process to put into place. My inner greedy miser threw a massive fit as I was considering doing this, and my limiting voices were shouting at the top of their lungs:

- "You're going to need every penny and more!"
- "You're going to run out of money and lose everything!"
- "You're not going to have enough!"
- "You can't afford to do that!"
- "What if something unforeseen comes up?"
- "They don't really *need* it!"
- "It's not your responsibility!"
- "It doesn't need to be a percentage, just give occasionally, when you can!"

I'm sure you have your own limiting voices, even as you read this chapter, and I'm sure that I can come up with many more myself. Here's the thing, though. I don't give because I'm spiritual; I don't give because I'm enlightened. I don't even give because I have a deep empathy for helping others.

That's part of it, sure. I believe in and care about the people I give to, but that's not the primary reason I created this practice; my reasoning is more practical and less altruistic. I created the practice because I came to understand that selfishly it's the best practice for personal freedom against the tyrannical rule of my inner greed and the scarcity mindset. I've rehearsed this poverty, lack-of-resources mindset so much in my life that it's easy for me to fall back into it. I need to give far more than the people and causes I contribute to need me to give. Those people and causes will be fine without my money, but my soul won't be fine if I hold onto money as if it were oxygen.

When I finally acted, in spite of my limiting voices, I was surprised to find that it felt great to give—really great. It was fun to give. It's fun and exciting to set this money aside and decide throughout the day or week how to go above and beyond for others; it could be with tips or birthday presents or helping family or buying meals for the homeless—the possibilities are endless. It's a fun way to systematically be extravagant toward others. I found that once the percentage has been set aside I almost feel like I'm giving away someone else's money, since it never felt like mine to begin with. I divided it out off the top before factoring it into my personal costs.

And best of all, it is a systematic and practical way to keep greed at bay and enjoy the benefits of the worldview that our resources are not just for us but also for sharing lavishly with others. This isn't to say that my wife and I don't save money and invest; we do, but we make sure that we build generosity into the fabric of our lives by building it into our budget, because being generous is a discipline. It's a way of being that is created through intention and systematic action. It's a built-in way to live in the question, "How can I contribute?" all the time, and this way of being has a tendency of spilling over into the other areas of our lives.

Acts of generosity and contribution infuse us with energy and joy, both of which are worth their weight in gold when it comes to productivity and creativity.

It changes our ways of being. New Dreamers understand that success is attained by asking ourselves how we can contribute to the world, seeking not what we can get but what we can give. Somehow, this is the way we not only increase our own success but also serve the world—creating a deeper sense of joy, peace, and purpose along the way.

What are some ways that you could intentionally build generosity and contributions into your life? Do this not as something that you *have* to do or feel like maybe you *should* do, but in a practical way that will allow you to experience the benefits of it. Do this to be even freer from greed and the scarcity mindset, and to create a way of being that becomes more resourceful in attaining your dreams while serving the world in the process. Are you willing to write down one consistent practice of generosity that you'd like to commit to for the next thirty days? Are you willing to start today?

PART 6

FINISHING STRONG

25

Finding Your Voice

If you want to be truly successful
invest in yourself to get the knowledge you need
to find your unique factor. "
~SIDNEY MADWED

One of the most common requests I've gotten over the years from my SSM students is, "Can you help me to sound like _____ (fill in the blank with the student's favorite singer/artist)?" I always give them pretty much the same answer: "I can make you sound like the best YOU possible, but I have no way, or desire, to help you sound like any other singer. I don't think that would serve you well, even if I were able to do so."

This, I'm sure, is not a particularly satisfying answer from my students' perspective, but it comes from a deep conviction that each one of us has a unique voice—both literally and figuratively—and it's that voice that is going to have the greatest impact on the world. The world doesn't need a replica of any other human being no matter how great that person's voice may be.

When I was eighteen or nineteen years old and living in San Diego, I responded to an advertisement to try out for an established band that was looking for a new singer. The individuals in the band came over to my apartment and listened to me play guitar and sing a few songs. They were sufficiently impressed and thought that I was a potentially good fit, so they scheduled a time for me to come over to their studio and do an audition rehearsal with full instrumentation.

At the time I was going through a Classic Rock phase and was listening to a lot of The Doors. I liked the lead singer Jim Morrison's voice partially because he, like me, was a baritone (bari-tenor, really). So, when the other band members asked me what songs I knew the lyrics to, I told them, "The Doors." They began playing the a song by The Doors, and I sang along.

One of the things I had prided myself on at the time was that I was a really good mimic. I could do a good Jim Morrison impression, so that's what I did. We finished that song and then we worked on another song from The Doors. Again, I did my best Morrison impression and felt like I killed it. I was happy about my performance and my voice and was pretty convinced that I had done a strong audition.

The bandleader drove me home later that evening, and, of course, I was eager to hear what he and the rest of the band thought. He started by telling me that he really liked my voice, but he and the rest of the guys felt that my voice sounded *too* much like Jim Morrison and that it would be difficult to market the band's sound. I couldn't believe it. I tried to explain that I was mimicking Morrison's voice on purpose and that I could sing differently, but it was too late. They had already made up their minds.

The truth of the matter was that I hadn't really developed my own voice quite yet, and if I weren't mimicking him, I would just switch to mimicking someone else.

That was a major turning point for me as a singer. I came to terms with the fact that I had a lot of fear about developing my own voice, thinking that it wasn't special enough or good enough to really make a splash—one of the limiting voices that kept me from attempting to develop my own voice for many years.

It was then that I began to write my own songs, and it was through writing my own songs that I found my unique voice. Instead of trying to sing like someone else, I just sang from my heart the songs that were meaningful to me. After a few years this eventually led to coffee shop performances, bar performances, tours, the production of several records, and a decent living as a singer/songwriter/musician for over a decade. I was playing for crowds with my own voice now. I was no longer a mimic but an artist.

Finding and honing your voice takes time. And this is true whether it's your singing voice or your figurative voice of contribution to the world—your unique style, personality, and mode of service to humanity through your talents and desires.

Steve Martin, in his book, *Born Standing Up*, says, "I did stand-up comedy for 18 years. Ten of those years were spent learning, four years were spent refining, and four years were spent in wild success." It takes time. And that's okay. Most of us feel like time is passing us by and it's too late for us—all of which are just limiting voices that we grab onto to keep us safe from the risk of pursuing the voice of our dreams.

Finding and developing our voices always starts the same way—with a choice. We often get stuck on what it is that we might be good at or what has the greatest chance of success or who we know that could get us a head start in a job that could make us good money. While there is a measure of wisdom to that way of thinking, it's starting from a non-resourceful place; it's backwards; it's asking the wrong question from the start. It's starting from a place of *doing* and not *being*. When we start from *being* we decide what it is that we want first. We choose what we want to be at the outset and then function as if it's true. We then take the next smallest step toward our goals and continue to take one small step after another everyday.

This was precisely the path of Steve Martin. He decided that he was a comic and began pursuing that dream on his unique path. He goes on to say, "The course was more plodding than heroic: I did not strive valiantly against doubters but took incremental steps studded with a few intuitive leaps."

Once we choose what our paths are, we simply take the next small step and stay on that path. We have the opportunity to switch onto a different path down the line, if we want, but we remain stuck and immobile until we choose a path. We can sit and think ourselves to death for a decade or two, or we can get into action now and discover quickly what we're passionate about—what we're willing to work hard toward no matter how much time it takes.

I remember when I was first contemplating going to college. A big part of me just wanted to start working or traveling and think about school later. One of my mentors at the time said, "Well, you can be thirty years old with a degree or without one." I enrolled for college that very week.

It doesn't matter how old you are or how old you're going to be when you have polished your unique contribution to the world and attained your dreams; you can either be twenty or forty or sixty, not having put the work in, and have the associated regrets, or you can begin plodding along the path today, make small incremental steps toward that goal, and look back and be glad you did.

The truth is that you are enough. There is so much more in you than you realize. You have gifts and strengths that others recognize in you that you're not even aware of yet. Be *you*, because there is no singer (or teacher, dancer, entrepreneur, or painter) like you, and you are uniquely priceless and uniquely brilliant.

You may be just starting out on the path, or you may still be stuck in indecision, or you may already have experienced a great deal of success. My question to you is, what's next? Where will your contribution be? Are you willing to make a decision today? Are you willing to take action on an idea that you have either been putting off or that you haven't had the courage or "time" to pursue? The truth is that we all have the same amount of time and choose to put time into our priorities, so when we say we don't have time, we're really just saying that whatever we "don't have time for" is simply not a priority right now; it's something we haven't committed to yet.

The voice of your dreams is calling to you, but it can be hard to hear when the voices of limitation are shouting so much louder. New Dreamers choose. New Dreamers get tired of waiting around for the perfect opportunity and instead get busy today with a small step toward the voices of their dreams and the paths that seem right. If they choose the wrong path, no problem. You can always course-correct.

Are you willing to believe that you are enough and that you have an invaluable contribution to offer the world, and that it's in that contribution that you will likely find your greatest success (and not to mention your greatest sense of fulfillment)? What is the next smallest step that will put you (back) on the path today? Are you willing to take it?

26

Completion

"Do not plan for ventures
before finishing what's at hand."
~Euripides

Finding my *singing* voice began when I started writing songs, but writing songs was a challenge for me. I would get really excited about an idea that I had for a song and spend some focused time and energy writing the parts that I was inspired to write. But there was always a lull in the writing of a song after the initial fire and inspiration wore off, so I would start writing a new song with any new rush of inspiration that I had, while leaving the previous song unfinished. After a while I had dozens and dozens of half-written or almost-finished songs but very few complete ones that I could actually perform.

Noticing this pattern, I told myself that I wouldn't start a new song until I finished the current song I was working on. This was tough because this final part of writing the song took extreme focus, a concentration that didn't feel like a creative process but more like grinding out desk job work—the kind of labor I didn't feel like doing.

As I began to think about it, I realized that writing and finishing a song was analogous to nearly all the projects in my life. It seemed that there was always an excitement or some form of inspiration at the outset of a project but that each project, at some point along the way, hit a point where the momentum and newness of the project wore off, and all that was left was a half-done project and a decision to continue or not. This slowing down of inspiration and progress usually came in the form of some kind of obstacle that seemed to challenge my commitment to the project, which revealed the story that I was believing and living in. If I were living in the story of, "This seems like a fun idea, and I'd like to get it done, as long as it doesn't take too much time or effort," then I would likely not complete the project and move onto the next project that piqued my interest. If the story I was living in was, "I'm committed to finishing this thing no matter what obstacles come my way. It's that important to me," then the chances of finishing grew exponentially. But it nearly always came down to a decision to take on the inspiration-lacking and seemingly non-creative work that was required to finish a project.

Once I finished writing that song before starting another one, I discovered a few things.

First, I was infused with energy and inspiration after completing the song. I felt so…complete. What seemed like it was going to drain my energy actually infused me with a fresh energy and excitement that I didn't get from my half-finished songs.

I got the opposite from the incomplete songs. Those ones I carried around with me as unfinished business that fatigued me because they came with the story, "I never finish what I start. What's wrong with me? I'll never be successful, since I'm not good at carrying things to completion." Those were just limiting voices; they didn't represent who I truly was. It was simply who I had chosen to be up until that point because of a habit I had gotten into; it was a story that I was taking to be true and living by as if it were reality.

The second thing I found was that I was a much more prolific songwriter when I stuck to my guns of completion. I was able to churn out song after song. I remember one summer I wrote twenty-five completed songs, and it was in that batch that I wrote one of the songs that became a crowd favorite for many years. I would either finish writing a song or I would decide that it wasn't a good enough song to spend the time completing. Either way, my mind was freed up from carrying around a bunch of unfinished songs. It was either completed by being placed in the trash bin or by finishing it. One way or another, I didn't have to think about it anymore and make up stories about myself regarding how I was defective from birth or wasn't raised right and didn't have the capacity to persevere and complete projects.

Third, my confidence in myself grew and grew as I completed more. The more songs I brought to completion, the more I confirmed that I was able to finish them and the more I chose to write, since I trusted myself to follow the song through to completion and have an actual product to offer to an audience or put on a record.

This confidence bled into other areas of my life as well. With a greater sense of trust in myself that I would follow through, I took more risks and would also take on bigger projects.

These New Dreamer principles apply to our everyday lives and our daily to-do lists. All the things left undone on our to-do lists have a way of draining our energy because we carry them around with us as unfinished business. We finish our workdays and continue to think about all that still needs to be done, and we feel tired, overwhelmed, behind, and like we can't seem to catch up.

Part of this comes from a misunderstanding of the principle of completion. We don't realize that completing tasks on our to-do list—our small steps toward the greatness that we're creating in our lives—will infuse us with new, fresh energy. Instead we feel like it's going to drain us if we complete the task. Then we feel tired before we even get started and say to ourselves, "I don't think I have the energy to work on that right now. I'm exhausted." We fail to realize that we're exhausted because these tasks are not done and we're overwhelmed by an oversized mental list of unfinished business.

So, instead of doing what we need to do, we have a tendency to avoid it, which leads to a greater sense of fatigue. This procrastination begets procrastination because it continues to produce a feeling of fatigue and even guilt.

But if we simply choose—robotically—to tackle the things we have to do, we will end the day with a greater amount of energy—not less energy. In fact, we're likely to have more energy at the end of a completed to-do list than before we started working on it.

We think that we're conserving our much-needed energy for a big task that may arise, so instead of doing the small things on our to-do lists, we avoid them and feel even more fatigued.

It wasn't until I made the connection between completion and energy, completion and productivity, and completion and confidence that I began to see my daily tasks differently. And when we complete the small tasks consistently and daily, then eventually big things occur. This is how it works for everyone.

The other benefit of the New Dreamer concept of completion is reduced anxiety and fear. Since all fear comes from picturing the future, and all future tasks seem bigger and scarier than they really are, as we tackle and complete tasks and projects, we decrease the anxiety and fears surrounding those projects and instead infuse ourselves with energy and power.

What is left undone in your life right now? Are you willing to write down five to ten things that you're willing to commit to completing? Are you willing to robotically tackle every item on your to-do list tomorrow and gauge how you feel afterward? Are you willing to increase your confidence in yourself by systematically completing all the projects in your life? What bigger projects might you be willing to take on if you had more confidence in yourself?

The way we engage with and complete our tasks today is a microcosm of how we engage with our lives as a whole. Thus, completing your most important steps today and then doing the same tomorrow is how we turn our lives into inspirations and masterpieces and how we stay on the path toward success.

Nice work. You've completed reading this book. How is your energy level right now?

Would You Do Me a Favor?

If you enjoyed *The Voice of Your Dreams* would you mind taking a minute and writing a review on Amazon? Even a short review helps, and it'd mean a lot to me.

If someone you care about is stuck in life or you think they would benefit from these New Dreamer principles, please send him or her a copy of this book. Whether you gift it to them on Amazon or email a copy of the PDF, either way would be great with me.

If you'd like to order copies of this book for your company, organization, or group of friends, please go to **www.thevoiceofyourdreams.com**.

Finally, if you'd like to get free bonus materials from this book and receive updates on my future projects you can sign up for my email list at www.thevoiceofyourdreams. com. **You can also follow me on Twitter and Instagram @ AaronAnastasi.**

The voice your dreams is calling to you…will you answer the call?

Acknowledgments

First, I want to thank Adrian Koehler. Without him this book would not have been possible. So much of my personal transformation chronicled in this book is a direct result of his powerful coaching. Adrian, my life is light-years better as a result of having met you. You are an exceptional coach, and I'm proud to call you a friend. My wife, Martha, whom I love with all my heart and who tolerated me talking about the content and direction of the book incessantly (obsessively) for a year.

I also want to thank my beta readers who helped me significantly raise the level and quality of this book's content and flow: Brilliant writer, Anike Tourse—my very first beta reader; Jordan Shappell—who also stayed up into the wee hours of the night with me helping me physically rearrange the chapters of the book that were printed and spread out on my office floor. Also, Anthony Chiles, Autumn "Fladmo" Smith, Hank Fortener, Jeff Holder, Matt Dalton, Britney Dalton, Jordan Owen, Shannon Taylor—who read it three times—Kelly Johnson, and Christie McGuire. Thank you all for your honesty and your time. I'm indebted to you.

To my rock star book launch team Morgan Owen, Meg Miller, and Johnny Young. I'm so grateful to you guys. Also part of the launch team is Chas Smith and Matt Smith, the best business partners and friends and guy could ever ask for and the ones who journeyed with me as co-founders of SSM. Dane Sanders, who coached me through the process of finishing the book and transitioning into the launch—incredibly helpful. Thank you, Dane.

To those who influenced me along the way: Steve Chandler, whose books gave me the courage and motivation to begin this book. Werner Erhard, Byron Katie, and Dan Tocchini, whose ideas made this book possible. Andy Stanley, a mentor and friend whose teachings and life shaped my young adulthood.

To my young but brilliant editor Chelsea Richardson.

To my New Dreamer friends I respect enormously who believed in me and my book enough to endorse it with blurbs: Robert Allan Ackerman, Cress Williams, Josiah Hawley, Nathan Chapman, David Magidoff, Wayne Miller, Greg Ullery, and Matt Mugford.

About the Author

Aaron Anastasi was born in Orange County, California —surfing, playing guitar, and performing musical theater. With a love for adventure, Anastasi was a pro snowboarder in Vail, Colorado, scaled Glacier Lake mountains in Bolivia, and cut pathways through the jungles of Contagem, Brazil. While pursuing his degrees in Humanities at Lee University (B.A.) and Princeton (M.Div.), he spent summers and weekends touring widely and performing music, sketch, and stand up comedy. Now he resides in Los Angeles, California where he works as a writer, actor, life coach, and producer. He also hosts the globally recognized "Superior Singing Method," an online singing lesson program that he created. His other online businesses include "Superior Songwriting Method," "Play Worship Guitar" and "Signing Success."

CPSIA information can be obtained
at www.ICGtesting.com
Printed in the USA
LVOW12s1016190917

548589LV00001BA/17/P